Complete Beginner's Guide to

WORD
For Windows

Jane Koch and
Jarrad McWilliams

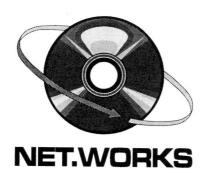

NET.WORKS

NET.WORKS

**Net.Works, PO Box 200
Harrogate, N.Yorks
HG1 2YR   England
Email: sales@net-works.co.uk
UK Fax: 01423-526035**

Net.Works is an imprint of Take That Ltd.

Published in association with Maximedia Pty Ltd
PO Box 529 Kiama, NSW 2533, Australia.

ISBN: 1 873668 43 0
© 1998 Take That Ltd. & Maximedia Pty Ltd

First Edition March 1998

10 9 8 7 6 5 4 3 2 1

Throughout this book you will find screen shots taken from Word for Windows. Unfortunately there are differences between the various releases of Word and a comprehensive catalogue of possibilities is beyond a publication of this size. Where there are major differences we have attempted to take these into consideration. However, there may be some screen shots which you do not recognise. We hope this does not spoil your enjoyment of the book.

Contents

Introduction

Did you know that today's word processors are capable of much more than traditional typewriters? Better still, you no longer need a range of software packages to create fantastic-looking work — rather, a single word processing program, such as Microsoft Word, can meet many (if not all) of your personal and business needs.

Using Microsoft Word you can quickly and easily improve the appearance of your documents, or even create complex brochures and newsletters. For those people who need help with grammar or spelling, Word offers document checking tools to help you work accurately, and the many other functions Word offers can quickly make your work look professional.

Many people have had some experience with a word processor, but are still unfamiliar with many of the functions it offers and treat it simply as an on-screen typewriter. However, word processing offers much more, and can save you time and improve the appearance and professionalism of your documents dramatically.

This book teaches you how to use Microsoft Word effectively, using easy-to-follow, step-by-step instructions. **The examples shown are based on one of the latest versions of the program - Word 97 - and if you are using Word 95, Word 6, Word 7 or an earlier version you may find that some of these look slightly different to the screens that appear on your computer.** Indeed you may have chosen not to install all possible option when you put the program on your computer. However, the concepts and the basic features each version offers are similar, and the hint boxes will let you know when to expect something different.

To get the most from this book, it is best to use it while sitting at your computer, so you can work through each function as it is introduced. Sit in a comfortable chair in a well-lit room, and angle your screen so that there is no glare on it. In addition, try to take a short break from computing every hour or so.

By following the explanations and step-by-step instructions in this book, you will be up to speed with Word in no time.

> ### QUICK TIP
> *If you need help, press the F1 function key to open the Help window.*

What is word processing?

The term "word processing" refers to the manipulation of text. A word processor is a software program that allows you to manipulate text using a computer. For example, using a word processor you can copy text and paste it somewhere else in your document, check your spelling and improve the presentation of your work.

Prior to the use of computers, documents were typed using typewriters. There are many differences between using a typewriter and a word processor. For example, when using a typewriter you must press the carriage return to begin a new line. Word processors such as Microsoft Word offer a **word-wrap** feature which automatically begins a new line when your text reaches the edge of the page shown on your screen. The only time you need to press the **Enter key** is to begin a new paragraph. You will become familiar with other differences between typewriters and word processors throughout this book.

> ## QUICK TIP
>
> *Keep a tray near your computer to recycle unwanted printouts. They can become scrap paper for the kids or just jotting paper for your own use.*

Using a Word Processor

Word processing involves four basic steps:

1.   Creating a document

Using a word processor is easier if you forget that you are using a computer. Simply think of your screen as a blank page which is ready to type on.

To create a document (such as a letter, memorandum or report) in your word processor, simply begin typing in the text, which will appear in a line across the screen. A blinking cursor shows your current position on the screen.

2.   Editing and formatting

This is an important step, as an edited and well-formatted document looks more professional than one that has been hastily put together.

Word processors enable you to create professional-looking documents by offering tools which allow you to check grammar and spelling, as well as formatting options which are used to set your text in bold or italics, or even increase or decrease text size. You will learn how to use formatting options throughout this book.

3.   Saving and retrieving (opening)

Once you have completed your document, you can "save" it - this means that you keep it stored safely on a disk - for later retrieval and re-editing. *Saving and retrieving is explained in-depth in Chapter 3.*

4.   Printing

Printing allows you to have a "hard copy" - a paper printout - of the document.

You will master each of these steps using the examples and information provided in this book. Word processing is not difficult, but it is important to learn how to get the most from your word processor. With a little practice, you will soon be using Microsoft Word to create professional-looking documents that will help you communicate your message more effectively.

'Cheat Sheet'

To help you get up to speed with Microsoft Word you will find a "cheat sheet" at the back of this book.

This handy reference guide lists the most commonly used **short cuts** in Word. Keep this sheet handy to access short cuts at a glance, making it easy to get the most out of Word.

Chapter 1

The Keyboard and Mouse

Your keyboard is used to type text and to access many of the functions offered by software programs. (The appearance of your keyboard may differ slightly from the picture shown below, but the basic layout and keys will be essentially the same.)

Pressing the **Caps Lock** key causes any letters you type to appear in capitals until you press it again. When the Caps Lock key is on the indicator in the top right hand corner of the keyboard lights up. To turn the Caps Lock key off and continue typing in lower case, simply press the key again.

The **Shift key** increases the number of functions or commands a standard keyboard can access. Most of these are similar to using the Shift key on a typewriter: for example, if you hold down Shift while pressing the number three (3) on your keyboard, a pound sign (£) will appear; similarly, holding down Shift while pressing the "a" key will display a capital "A".

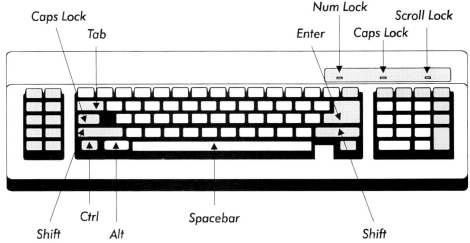

Figure 1.1: A standard keyboard.

The Shift key differs from the Caps Lock key in that it only affects what you type while it is held down.

Like Shift, the **Ctrl** ("control") key gives other

keys a new "job" while it is held down. For example, you can print your document in Microsoft Word by holding down Ctrl and pressing "p". These "jobs" are often called **functions**, and throughout this book you will find explanations of the functions you will use to create your documents.

The **Alt** ("alternate") key allows quick access to menus (lists of functions that Word can perform). For instance, holding down Alt while pressing the letter "f" in Microsoft Word activates the File pull-down menu. Using Alt is a handy alternative to using the mouse.

Pressing the **Tab** key moves the cursor across your screen at preset intervals, just as the Tab key on a typewriter does. Each time you press the Tab key the cursor moves at a preset interval, but this setting can be changed. Tabs are an easy, accurate way to align text. (*You will discover how to use tabs to organise your text in Chapter 4.*)

The **spacebar** inserts a blank space between characters, for instance to separate words and sentences.

The **Enter** key (often called the **Return** key) is used to begin a new paragraph. Enter can also be used to confirm a command. Often Word will check whether you really want it to perform a command, offering options such as YES, NO and OK. Usually pressing Enter tells Word to go ahead and perform the command.

The Function keys, which range from **F1 to F12**, are usually located across the top of the keyboard. These keys are used to perform commands or functions. For example, pressing the F1 key in Microsoft Word activates Help. You will learn how to use several of the function keys later in this book.

As their names suggest, the **Page Up** and **Page Down** keys allow you to move up or down through your document one page at a time. These keys are very useful when you are working with several pages of text, as they allow you to easily move through the document. (If your document is only one page long, these keys move the cursor to the top and bottom of the page respectively.)

The **Delete** key deletes one character to the right of the cursor each time you press it. Delete is used to remove mistakes or unwanted characters.

Backspace is similar to Delete, but differs in that it removes characters one at a time to the left of the cursor. The Backspace key is often represented simply as an arrow, and is usually located above the Enter key.

In versions 6 and 7 of Microsoft Word when pressed once the **Insert** key replaces existing text with new text as it is typed. For this reason, it is also known as the **Typeover** or **Overwrite** key. To turn Insert off and return to normal typing mode (where new text is automatically inserted between existing words), press Insert again. In Word 97, this feature works only by double-clicking on the **OVR** button on the status bar *(this is explained fully in Chapter 3)*.

The Cursor Control keys (also known as the **Arrow keys**) are marked with small arrows and situated at the far right of the keyboard. (Many keyboards have a second set of arrow keys between the main set of keys and the Numeric Keypad; they work the same way.) The Left Arrow moves the cursor one character to the left each time it is pressed, similarly, the Right Arrow moves the cursor one character to the right at a time. The Up and Down Arrow keys move the cursor one line up or down respectively each time they are pressed.

Pressing the **Home** key moves your cursor to the beginning of the line your cursor is in. Pressing the End key moves your cursor to the end of that line.

The Num Lock key enables you to use the numbers on the Numeric Keypad. When Num Lock is activated, a small indicator light on the top right of the keyboard lights up. To turn Num Lock off and continue using the keys as cursor control keys, press the key again.

The **Esc**ape key is used to reply in the negative to a question that Word asks. For example, if Word asks you to confirm whether you would like to print a document, pressing Esc will cancel the printing.

QUICK TIP

To see the name of a button on a button-bar, rest your pointer on it and the button name will appear.

The Mouse

A mouse is a pointing device that allows you to input instructions into the computer.

It is important not to confuse the mouse pointer with the blinking line (the "cursor") that indicates where your typing will appear. Using the mouse you can move a pointer (which appears as a small arrow or **I-beam**) to any position on your screen - only by clicking once with one of the mouse buttons do you move the cursor to that position or perform an action. For example, you can move the mouse pointer to the menu bar at the top of the screen, but nothing will actually happen until you click one of the mouse buttons.

In Microsoft Word the left mouse button is used most often; therefore, always click with your left mouse button unless otherwise instructed.

You can also use the mouse to reposition the blinking cursor that Word uses to show where your typing will appear. Move the mouse pointer to the place in the document you want to type, and click the left mouse button. The blinking cursor will move to the same place.

Chapter 3 explains other ways you can use the mouse to work with your document.

NOTE

Some of the mouses available today come with three mouse buttons. The third button is not used in Word, and is usually only required by drawing or graphics programs.

Chapter 2

The Word Screen

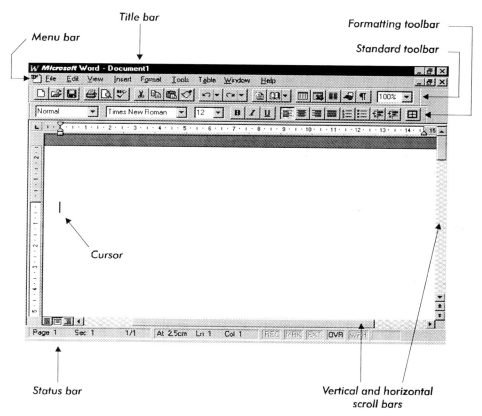

Menu bar

Title bar

Formatting toolbar

Standard toolbar

Cursor

Status bar

Vertical and horizontal scroll bars

The Microsoft Word screen is easy to understand and intuitive to use. The main parts of the Word screen are shown in the figure, above, and discussed in this chapter.

Title bar

The coloured bar at the top of the Word screen is the title bar. The title bar displays the program in use (Microsoft Word) in the left-hand corner. The name of the document you are working on (in this case, Document1) appears beside the program name.

Menu bar

The menu bar is located directly under the title bar and contains the menu names, such as File, Edit and View.

Clicking once on a menu name will open a pull-down menu, which offers a series of options. For instance, the File menu is shown right:

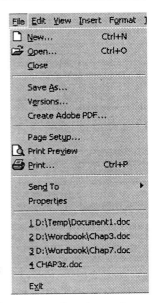

Toolbars

Situated just below the menu bar are the toolbars (shown in figure 2.1).

These are also known as button bars, as the **icons** (little pictures) they display are shown on small buttons. Clicking on an icon provides a shortcut to a commonly-used feature of Microsoft Word.

 The icons usually depict their function: for example, the printer button (left) shows a picture of a printer. You can print your document by simply clicking on this icon.

Dialog boxes

Often when you are using an option from the menu bar or a toolbar, Microsoft Word will display a small box on your screen requesting further information. Sometimes this dialog box contains "drop-down menus", which appear when you click on a small down-pointing arrow beside an option. These menus allow you to choose from several options.

Occasionally a menu or dialog box will contain an option that is "greyed out" — you can see it, but it looks like it's had a grey film laid over it. This means that the option is not available in this situation, although it can be available at other times.

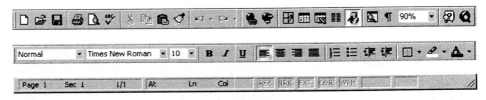

Figure 2.1 The standard toolbar (top), the formatting toolbar (centre) and the status bar (bottom) are all important parts of the Word screen.

Rulers

The rulers can be seen along the top and the left-hand side of the Word screen, as shown below:

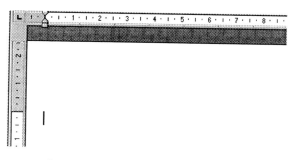

Rulers indicate page boundaries. The white, numbered sections on each ruler show the area of the page within which you can type, and the grey numbered sections define the blank areas that form the page margins.

To display (or hide) the rulers, use the mouse to move your cursor to the word "View" on the menu bar and click once to display the View menu.

When the Ruler command is active — that is, when you can see the rulers on the screen — you will see a small tick beside the word "Ruler". If there is no tick, clicking on the word "Ruler" will display the rulers (and add a box with a tick in it next to "Ruler"). Clicking on it again will remove the tick, and the rulers will no longer be visible.

The units of measurement marked on the ruler can be changed using the Tools menu.

Simply move your cursor to the word "Tools" and click once. From the pull-down menu select Options, then click on the tab marked "General". In the box that appears, use the drop-down menu titled "Measurement units" to select either inches, centimetres, points or picas. (Points and picas are terms used in the graphics industry to measure, respectively, font size and distance.)

QUICK TIP

Before changing any of Word's settings, write down the original settings — just in case you need to change them back.

Scroll bars

The vertical scroll bar, which is situated along the right hand side of the Word screen, allows you to move quickly through the document.

This is called "scrolling" because it appears that the document is being rolled past your eyes as if it is written on a scroll.

The horizontal scroll bar, at the bottom of your screen, enables you to pan across the page.

You can scroll through a document by dragging the small box within the bar, or by clicking on the scroll buttons (which are marked with arrows and situated at the ends of the bars).

To move around your document quickly, click on the "blank" areas of the scroll bars. This will scroll through large sections of the document at a time.

Status bar

The status bar (shown in figure 2.1 on page 12) is located at the bottom of your screen.

Information relating to the page you are working on (such as page number) is displayed on the status bar.

The status bar also alerts you to other changes that are occurring within your document; for example, while your document is being saved a small disk icon will appear on the status bar.

Cursor

The cursor, which looks like a small blinking line, indicates where on the screen the next character you type will appear.

The cursor is primarily used to edit text; for example, text can be highlighted using the cursor and then deleted or moved. You should constantly be aware of the position of your cursor when working in Microsoft Word.

Managing Windows

While working with Word, you can have several different windows (dialog boxes) open within your Word screen.

It is important to know how to manage these windows using the Minimise, Maximise and Close buttons, which are located in the upper right-hand corner of the Word screen, as shown in the following diagram:

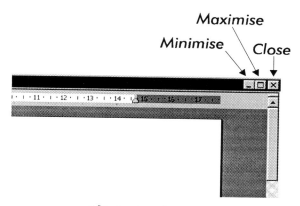

Minimise button

Clicking on this button, which resembles a small horizontal line, hides the window, although the program is still running. To restore Word, click on the Word button on the taskbar.

Maximise button

Clicking on the Maximise button, which looks like a small square, causes the Word screen to enlarge and fills the entire screen.

Restore button

When the screen is maximised the Maximise button becomes the Restore button.

This button, which is located in the upper right-hand corner of a maximised Word screen, resembles two overlapping windows. Clicking on this button restores the Word screen to the size it was before it is maximised.

Close button

The Close button, which looks like a small "X", can be seen in the upper-right hand corner of the Word screen and all dialog boxes which open within Word. Clicking on this button closes Word or any other window open within the Word screen.

Help

The Help menu can be invaluable when you are having difficulty in Word. From the Help menu you can access information about Word by searching for a particular topic or word, or by browsing through the contents of Help. To search for a particular topic using Help:

Help in Word 6 and 7

1. Click on **Help** on the menu bar.
2. In Word 6 from the pull-down menu click on **Search for Help on....** In Word 7.0, click on **Microsoft Word Help Topics** from the pull down menu, then select **Index**.

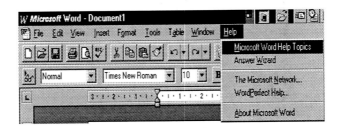

3. The **Help Topics: Word Help** dialog box will appear.

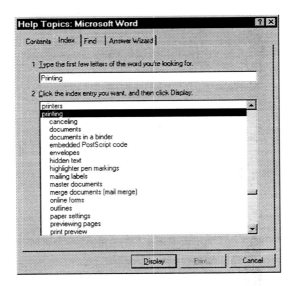

Type the words or topic you want help with into the text box marked with a "1"...

...and a list of headings or index entries related to this topic will appear in the list box in the section marked "2".

4. Choose a heading or index entry from the list in section 2.

5. Click on the **Display** button once you have chosen a topic.

   (For example, if you need help with printing a document, you would type the word "printing" in text box 1, then from Section 2 select the word "printing" and finally click on Display.)

6. Clicking on the Display button opens a dialog box which shows all the topics relevant to printing.

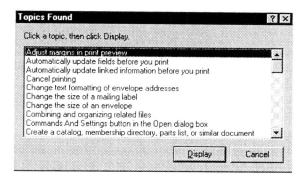

Select a topic and click on Display again to view a dialog box containing explanations about that topic.

Help in Word 97

1. Click on Help on the menu bar.

2. From the Help pull-down menu, click on "**Contents and Index**", shown below.

3. From the "Help Topics: Microsoft Word" dialog box, click on the **Index** tab.

4. Type the words or topic you want help with into the text box marked "1". A list of headings or index entries appears in the list box under section "2".

5. Choose a heading or index entry from this list by clicking on your selection with the mouse, or using the arrow keys to scroll through the topics. Once you have selected a topic, click on the **Display** button. A dialog box will appear listing the related topics found. From here simply click on a topic, then click Display.

The Help Button

The Help button on the toolbar (which has a question mark and an arrow on it) can be used to obtain a description of what each button on the toolbar does.

To use this option, click once on the Help button and then click on the button of your choice on the toolbar. This opens up a Help window which explains the functions of that button.

In Word 97

Clicking on the question mark in Word 97 calls up the Office Assistant (shown below) which asks the question: "What would you like to do?"

Type the topic you want to search for in the box, then click on **Search**.

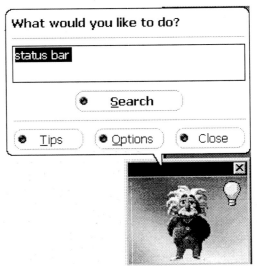

A window opens showing information relevant to that topic. For instance, a search for the topic "printing", will display the dialog box below:

Click on the button beside the topic in the list that you wish to view.

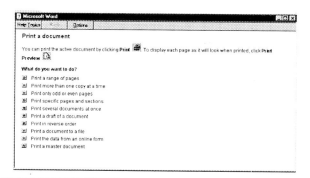

A window containing step-by-step information on that topic will appear, such as the one shown below:

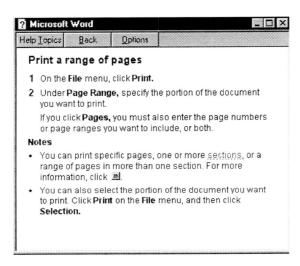

To close this window, click on the Close button, which looks like a small "**X**" in the top right-hand corner of the window.

Chapter 3

Creating and Editing Your Document

Before you begin writing, you will need to create a new Microsoft Word document. When you launch Microsoft Word for the first time, Word automatically creates a new document which is named *Document1*. If you open a second document it will be named *Document2*, a third will be called *Document3*, and so on. Note, however, that these names are only temporary — you can choose your own name for each document when you save it.

Creating a New Document

There are three ways to create a new document in Word. The most commonly used is explained below.

1. Click on **File** on the menu bar.
2. Select **New** from the pull-down menu.
3. In the New dialog box, note the word Normal is highlighted in the Template text box. This means that we are creating a Normal document.

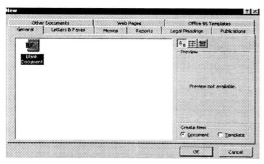

Word 97: New dialog box

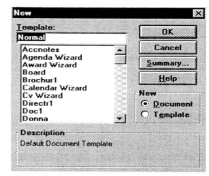

Word 6.0: New dialog box

Note that several templates and document wizards are listed under the Template list box. These prepared templates and wizards can be used to create brochures, newsletters and other professional looking

QUICK TIP

There are two other ways to open a new document. Either click on the **New** *button on the Standard toolbar, or use the keyboard combination* **Ctrl + N** *(hold down* **Ctrl** *while pressing the letter* **N***).*

documents. With the word *Normal* highlighted or *Blank Document* selected, click on **OK**.

4. Once you have created a document, you can begin typing. As you type your text will appear on the screen.

Entering and Editing Text

When you have typed in all your text, you are ready to edit it; that is, to correct, move, and add to what you've typed, and to delete any errors.

Read through your text carefully, checking for errors. Then using the cursor control keys (the arrow keys), or the mouse (*as described in Chapter 1*), move your cursor to those places in the document you want to change.

The most commonly used keys for editing and correcting are the arrow keys, Backspace, Delete, Enter and the spacebar. (*If you are not familiar with where these keys are and what they do, refer to Chapter 1.*)

Selecting Text

Often, you will need to make changes to more than one character at a time. For example, you may want to change the size of a large amount of text, make it all bold or italic, or delete an entire sentence quickly.

By selecting sections of text or paragraphs the changes you make will apply to the all the text you have highlighted.

There are several ways to select text, depending on whether you want to use your mouse, or keyboard. You will probably find it useful to use a combination of these methods.

Selecting text using the mouse

As you move your mouse pointer around the screen you will notice that it changes shape. When above menus, scroll bars, button bars and so on, it appears as a small arrowhead, but above text it changes to a large "**I**". This is called an **I-beam**, and it is used to select text.

Instructions

1. Position the I-beam in front of the word or words you want to select.

2. While holding down the left mouse button, drag the I-beam across the words. As you do this, you will notice that the words become highlighted (they change colour).

   Once you have highlighted all the words you wish the changes to apply to, release the mouse button. The words will remain highlighted.

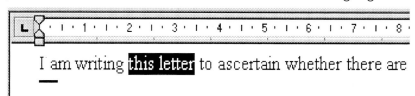

3. If you have selected the wrong words, don't panic. To cancel the selection (also called "de-selecting"), simply click once with the left mouse button anywhere on your page. The highlight will disappear and you can select again.

   You can also use the mouse to select single words or paragraphs. To select a word, place the I-beam anywhere on that word, and quickly click the left mouse button twice. To select an entire paragraph, place the I-beam anywhere within that paragraph, and click the left mouse button *three* times in quick succession.

Selecting text using the keyboard

If you do not have a mouse, or prefer to use your keyboard to select text, follow these instructions:

Instructions

1. Use the arrow keys to position the cursor in front of the text you want to select.

2. Press the **F8** (function key) once, then use the arrow keys to move the cursor to the end of the text you want to select. The text will be highlighted.

3. If you want to cancel your selection, press the **Esc**ape key once, then any of the arrow keys.

EXERCISE — Editing using Microsoft Word

Bill Shields
100 Sample Ave
❶ HarrogateHG1 2YR

20 April 1999

Ms P. Brown
Managing Partner
PO Box 588
Middlesbrough TS1 6EB

Dear Ms Brown:

I am writing to ascertain whether there are any vacancies within your
company. ❷ I have enclosed my resume, which illustrates my work
experience to date.

My present job is due to become redundant within a few months, and I
will be relocating back to my home town of Middlesbrough

If you have any vacancies that I ❸ would would be suitable for, please

do not hesitate to contact me for an interview.

Yours faithfully,

Bill Shields

❶ In the address at the top of the page, the word "Harrogate" and the postcode have been written as one word. To separate them, use the arrow keys or the mouse to move the cursor between the letters "e" and "H". Press the spacebar to separate the words.

❷ A new paragraph is needed following the first sentence of the first paragraph. To separate the first and second sentences into different paragraphs, move the cursor between the full stop and the letter "I" and press Enter twice.

❸ In the last paragraph, the word "would" is repeated. To remove one instance of this word, place the cursor in front of the "w" and press Delete six times (once for each letter of the word and one time to delete the extra space left between "would" and "be").

Alternatively, you can select text by positioning the cursor in front the text you wish to select, and holding down the Shift key while using the arrow keys to highlight your selection. To de-select, release Shift and press any of the arrow keys.

Formatting text

You can use formatting to make your document more interesting and communicate your message more effectively. Using bold, italic, or underlined text, changing font, and adjusting text alignment (also called "justification") can help you emphasise important points, organise your information, and improve readability.

In Word, text is formatted using the formatting toolbar shown below, or using the Format pull-down menu.

Changing the font

Typefaces (or character styles) are called "**fonts**". There are many different fonts available for use in Microsoft Word - each suitable for different uses. You may also acquire new fonts via different programs running under windows.

Font Name	*Sample of Font*
Staccato555	𝒮𝓉𝒶𝒸𝒸𝒶𝓉𝑜555
Times New Roman	Times New Roman
Zapf Dingbats	✳●□❖ ✦✸■✳☺♥▼▲

Using a different font for certain types of information (such as chapter headings) can make these stand out from the rest of the document.

NOTE

In Word 6 and 7, if you cannot see the formatting toolbar, click on View on the menu bar. From the View pull-down menu, click on Toolbars. In the Toolbar dialog box, click on the word Formatting or click inside the Formatting textbox, and click on OK. For Word 97 users, click on View, point to Toolbars, and from the pull-down menu click on the word Formatting. Remember that when there is a tick in front of the toolbar it is visible.

However, be aware that using too many different fonts in a document can make it look cluttered and amateurish. For a cleaner, more professional look, do not use more than two or three fonts in a document.

Instructions

1. Select the text you want to change.
2. Click on the down arrow beside the **Font** selection on your toolbar (this will show the name of the font that is currently being used). A menu which lists all the fonts that are available to you will appear. The section of the menu above the horizontal line shows the fonts already used in the document; the section below shows all the fonts available.)

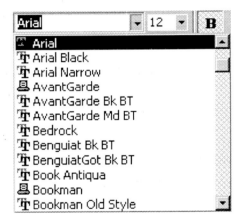

3. Click on the name of the font you want to use. The menu will disappear and the selected text changes to that font.

Alternatively you can change the font using the **Font** dialog box. This method has the advantage of allowing you to see a sample of the font before you apply it to the selected text.

Instructions

1. Select the text you want to change.
2. Click on **Format** on the menu bar.
3. From the Format pull-down menu, click on **Font**.
4. Choose the font style you like by clicking on the font name.
5. Click on **OK** to apply that font to the selected text, or choose a different font. Your text will not be changed until you click on **OK**.

Changing the size of text

The method used to change the size of your text is similar to changing the font.

Instructions

1. Select the text you want to change.

2. To the right of the Font section of the formatting toolbar, you will see a box with a number in it. This number is the size of the font, measured in "**points**". (The best way to understand points is to think of them as a measure of *relative* size: 12-point type is larger than 8-point type, for example. You will soon acquire a feel for which point size will suit the task at hand. This text is in 11-point.)

3. Click on the down arrow on the size section. A menu lists several sizes; however, you can stipulate any size by simply typing it into the size text box.

4. If you don't like the size you have chosen, simply choose a different size from the list or type in your choice and press Enter (the text remains selected until you click elsewhere in the document, so there is no need to re-select it).

Alternatively you can change the font size using the Font dialog box, which allows you to see a sample of the size before you change the text.

Instructions

1. Select the text you want to change.

2. Click on **Format** on the menu bar.

3. From the Format pull-down menu, click on **Font**.

4. Choose the font size you like by clicking on the appropriate number in the size box.

5. Click on **OK** to accept the changes you just made (or else choose a different size).

Bold, italic and underline

You can also change the way text looks by using **bold**, *italic* and underline.

Select the text you want to change, then click on any or all of the **Bold**, **Italic** or **Underline** buttons (shown below).

You can choose any combination of these — even all three at once. You will notice that when

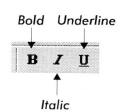

this formatting is applied to text, the appropriate button appears to be depressed.

To remove this formatting, select the text you want to change, then click on the appropriate button(s) again. The button(s) will "pop out", showing you that the selected text does not have that format applied.

If you prefer to use the keyboard to apply this formatting, follow these steps:

Instructions

1. Select the text you want to change.
2. Hold down the Ctrl key and press one of the following letters :

> **B** for Bold
> **U** for Underline
> **I**   for Italics

Justification (text alignment)

Justification refers to how your text is set within the left and right margins. If your text is aligned with the left margin, it is "left justified" (sometimes called "flush left"); text aligned with the right margin is "right justified" (or "flush right"); centred text is "centre justified"; and text aligned with *both* the left and right margins is "fully justified".

Headings are commonly centred using the centre justification button on the toolbar – a much faster, easier and more precise way of centring than using the spacebar or Tab key.

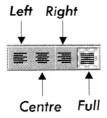

Instructions

1. Select the text you wish to justify.
2. Click on the button in the formatting toolbar that shows the justification you want.

The example below shows text justified in several ways. The heading is centred, the first paragraph left justified, the second paragraph right justified and text in the final paragraph has full justification applied.

The Land of the Forbidden

Lachlan and his friends walked for many days, crossing the rough mountain terrain leading to the distant country where lay the "Land of the Forbidden".

After many weeks of relentless walking, they finally came upon the "Land of the Forbidden". Hearts pounding with excitement, they entered the dark, dense forest.

The vegetation was thick and lush. All around them were hundreds of trees, growing thick and tall. Small animals scurried past. The forest was simply alive with activity.

Cut, Copy and Paste

An important advantage of word-processing over using a typewriter is that it allows you to move, duplicate or remove text without retyping your entire document. Removing text is called "cutting", and replacing it in the document is called "pasting". Duplicating text is known as "copying".

The Cut, Copy and Paste buttons (shown below) are situated on the formatting toolbar.

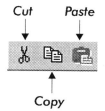

Cut   Paste

Copy

Instructions for cutting text

To remove text (either to move it to a different place or to delete it entirely):

1. Select the text that you want to remove.
2. Click on the **Cut** button in the formatting toolbar. The text will disappear (although Word will store a copy of it until the next time you use the Cut command).

To place cut text into the document:

Instructions for pasting text

1. Position your cursor in the document where you would like your text to reappear.
2. Click on the **Paste** button in the formatting toolbar. Your text will appear.

Instructions for copying text

To duplicate text (while leaving the original text in place):

1. Select the text that you would like to copy.
2. Click on the **Copy** button in the formatting toolbar.
3. Position your cursor in the document where you would like a copy of the text to appear.
4. Click on the **Paste** button; your text will appear where you positioned the cursor.

Instructions for using the keyboard

To use the keyboard, follow the same steps, but use the following keystrokes instead of the buttons on the formatting toolbar:

- To Copy: Hold down the **Ctrl** key and press **C**
- To Cut: Hold down the **Ctrl** key and press **X**
- To Paste: Hold down the **Ctrl** key and press **V**

Undo and Redo

At times you may change your mind about the formatting changes you have just made, or you may make a mistake. Mercifully, Word allows you to undo changes.

Instructions

1. Click on **Edit** on the menu bar. You will see the word "**Undo**", followed by the most recent action (for example, "Undo Cut" or "Undo Typing").

2. Click on **Undo**. The last change you made will disappear. The Undo command can reverse your actions multiple times. In the case that Word cannot reverse the last action the command changes to **Can't Undo**.

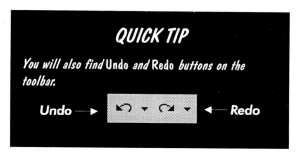

QUICK TIP

You will also find Undo *and* Redo *buttons on the toolbar.*

Undo ➝   ⬅ Redo

3. To redo undone changes, click on **Edit** in the menu bar. You will see the word "Redo", followed by the most recently undone action. Click on **Redo**.

You can use the keyboard instead of the menu bar.

Instructions for using the keyboard to Undo and Redo

1. Hold down the **Alt** key.
2. Press the **Backspace** key to undo changes.
3. To redo, hold down the **Ctrl** key and press the letter **Y**.

Saving your document

To store your document in order to later recall it, you must save it. It is a good practice to save your document on a regular basis, as unexpected occurrences such as power failures and computer problems can lead to the loss of data that has not been saved.

You can save your data to either your hard disk or to a floppy disk. The hard disk is commonly known as the C: drive, while the floppy disk is usually the A: drive.

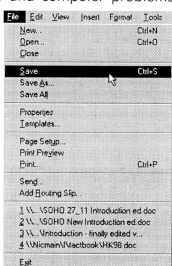

Instructions

1. To save a new document, click on **File** on the menu bar.
2. From the pull-down menu click on **Save**.
3. If the document has not been saved previously, the Save As dialog box appears, prompting you to give the document (also called a "file") a name.

4. Type a name for the document in the **File Name** text box.

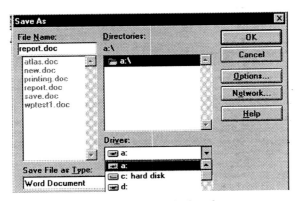

Word 6: Save As dialog box

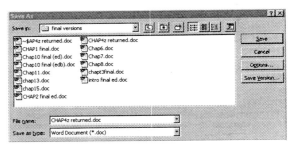

Word 7 and 97: Save As dialog box

Note that if you are using Word 7 for Office 95/97, your file name can be up to 255 characters long with spaces in between. For example if your document were the 1998 Financial Report, your file name could be: *1998 Financial Report for James Good Ltd.*

However, Word 2 and Word 6 only allow file names to be between one and eight characters long. You can use any letter or numeral, but you cannot use characters such ; : = < > [ ] ( ) \ / . ? or spaces in your file name. An example of a file name for a report titled "June Budget for 1998" could be *Junbgt98.* (You can use both capitals and lower case letters.)

5. Click on the **Save (OK)** button at the right-hand side of the dialog box. You will know that your document is saved when its name appears on

the title bar of your Word screen (see Chapter 2 for more information on the Word screen). For example, in the diagram below, the document name is *Report.doc*.

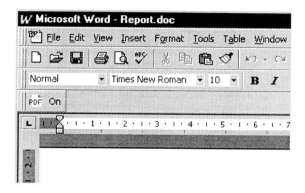

Important Notice

If you make any further changes to your document, you will want to save it again to ensure you do not lose these changes. Because you have already named your document, you will not be asked to name it each time you save. Word will save the updated document under the same file name.

Save As

If you wish to rename a document or save it to a different location, choose the **Save As** option from the Edit pull-down menu.

Example: Judy has to type two similar reports. To avoid retyping the document, she finishes the first document and saves it under the name *John*. She then edits the document and saves the edited document under a different file name *(Judy)*. To achieve this, she clicks on File, then selects the Save As command, which opens the dialog box. She types *Judy* in the file name text box.

Saving to a floppy disk

To save a copy of your work from your computer to your floppy disk, take the following steps:

1. To save a new document, click on **File** on the menu bar.
2. If the document hasn't been saved previously, select **Save** from the File pull-down menu. (If the document has been saved, click on **Save As** to open the dialog box.)

3. From the **Save In** drop-down box, select **Drive A:**.

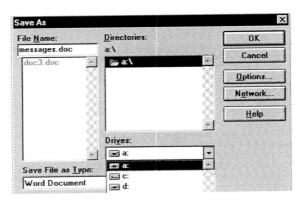

Word 6: Save In drop-down box

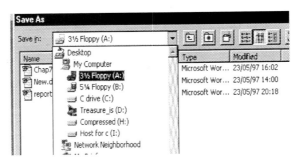

Word 7 and 97: Save In drop-down box

4. Click on the **Save (OK)** button to save the document to the floppy disk in drive A:.

Example: Judy wants to take home a copy of a report she has been working on at work. To do this, she clicks on **File** on the toolbar, then **Save As** so that she can specify the floppy drive as the destination of the saved document.

Closing a File

Once you have finished working on a file you will want to "close" it and put it away. There are two ways to close a file. Either use the menu bar by clicking on **File** then selecting **Close**, or use the keyboard by holding the Ctrl key and pressing F4.

Instructions

To close a document:
1. Click on **File** on the menu bar.
2. Select **Close** from the **File** pull-down menu.

When closing a document, Word will ask you if you wish to save any changes you made since you last saved the document. Click on *Yes* to save the changes. If you have not yet given the document a name, Word will open the Save As dialog box, prompting you to name the document.

Opening an existing file

You may want to open a file you created earlier to make some changes. To retrieve ("open") an existing document:

Instructions

1. Select **File** from the menu bar.
2. Click on **Open** to display the Open dialog box. All files in the open folder are displayed in the window.
3. Select the file you want to open by clicking on it. When it is selected the file name will be highlighted in blue.

QUICK TIP

You can also open an existing document by clicking on File *on the menu bar and selecting the file name from those at the bottom of the pull-down menu, where Word displays recently-saved documents. The document will only be listed if it has recently been in use.*

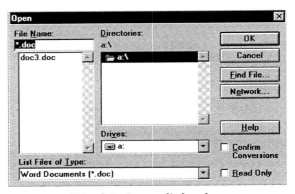

Word 6: Open dialog box

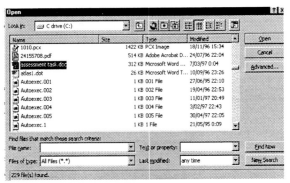

Word 7 and 97: Open dialog box

4. Click on Open (OK) to open the file.

Exiting from Word

If you attempt to exit Word before saving your document a dialog box will appear asking if you wish to save your changes. To do this, select Yes. If you choose No, Word closes without saving your work.

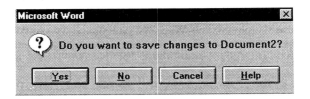

Instructions

To exit Word:
1. Click on **File** on the menu bar.
2. Select **Exit** from the pull-down menu. (Alternatively, you can use the key combination Alt+F4 or click on the "X" in the top right corner.)

Document Index

While you are learning Microsoft Word it is a good idea to keep track on paper of all the documents you have created, made a copy of, or stored on floppy disks. This will help you to locate your documents quickly. A sample document tracker, which you can photocopy and keep, is supplied here.

DOCUMENT TRACKER

Sheet Number: ....   **Your Name:** ....

Date	Filename (Document Name)	Subject/Details	Disk Number	Backed up (Copied to floppy)

Chapter 4

Formatting Your Document

In Chapter 3 you learned how to select and format text. This chapter will show you how to format your entire document. This includes indenting text, changing the spacing between lines, inserting a page break, inserting or adjusting tabs and borders, using "bullet points" and numbering to create lists, placing borders around (or shading behind) a paragraph, and many other options which will help to make your document more readable and interesting.

Viewing your document

Microsoft Word is a **WYSIWYG** ("what-you-see-is-what-you-get") word processor. This means that it can display your document on screen exactly as it will print.

However, Word also allows you to view your document in several different ways so that you can decide how best to format it.

Normal View

By default Word displays your document in Normal view mode. This allows you to see all your text, and is useful when you are editing and formatting text.

However, Normal view does not show headers, footers, columns, Clip Art, text boundaries or other document formatting characteristics. Therefore, to make the most of Word's features you may want to use another viewing option.

To change to Normal view or to check your current view setting:

1. Select **View** from the menu bar.
2. From the View pull-down menu, click on **Normal** if this option is not already selected.   A tick, a dot or a depressed button in front of an option indicates your current selection.

Page Layout view

Page Layout view displays your document in its entirety. Features like columns, headers, footers, and Clip Art are shown exactly as they will print.

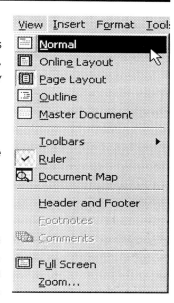

To change to Page Layout view:

1. Select **View** from the menu bar.
2. From the View pull-down menu, select **Page Layout**.

Outline view and Master Document view

Outline view and Master Document view are useful when working with lengthy documents, such as books or long reports. These organise work into major headings and sub-headings, and group related information.

Most word-processing users will only rarely need these features, but for those who work with lengthy documents these views can offer many advantages.

Outline view is used to organise long documents into mulit-level headings and sub-headings.

It allows users to structure ideas and plan documents by collapsing body text so that only headings and sub-headings are visible.

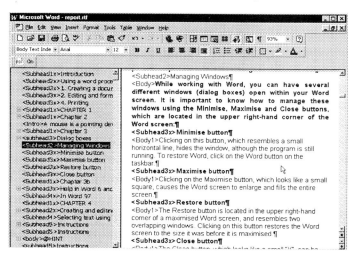

When Outline view is selected the Outline toolbar can be seen below the Formatting toolbar, and markers are visible on the left-hand side of the document.

QUICK TIP

To save on the cost of printing, always view your document in Print Preview before printing. Select **File** *from the Toolbar, then* **Print Preview.**

Master Document view allows users to hyperlink sub-documents. To work on an individual document you simply click on the link contained in the master document. This feature is particularly useful when working with several chapters of a book.

Selecting views:

1. Select **View** from the menu bar;
2. From the View pull-down menu, click on **Outline** or **Master Document**.

Online Layout View

Online Layout is a new viewing option offered in Word 97. In Online Layout view you can link information to a particular topic. When this topic is clicked on, you are taken to the related linked information. This is known as "**hyperlinking**", and is commonly used in multimedia and on the Internet.

Online Layout view also offers a navigation pane (referred to as a "Document Map"), visible as a shaded pane at the left of the document window. Clicking on a particular topic in the Document Map makes you immediately jump to that topic.

Zoom View

Zoom acts like a magnifying glass that can make your document look either larger or smaller. It is important to note, however, that the document's actual size, and the size at which it prints out, do not change when you use Zoom.

"Zooming in" - making the document look larger than its actual size - is perfect when you're having trouble seeing small text on the screen. "Zooming out" – making the document look smaller – is useful for getting an overall impression of how the document will look when it is printed.

To change the Zoom on your screen:

1. Select **View** from the menu bar.

2. From the View pull-down menu, click on **Zoom**.

3. In the **Percent** text box, click on the up arrow to increase your Zoom level, or on the down arrow to decrease it. A percentage greater than 100 will make the document appear larger; while a percentage less than 100 decreases its apparent size.

4. Alternatively, you can use Zoom by selecting an option under the **Zoom To** section:

- ● **Page Width** enlarges the document so that it is as wide as your document window,

- ● **Whole Page** fits one entire page into your document window, and

- ● **Two Pages (**or "Many Pages" in Word 97) fits two (or more) entire pages into your document window.

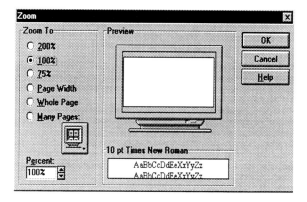

5. Click on **OK**.

The Zoom button

You can also change the zoom in Word 6, 7 and 97 by clicking on the Zoom button on the toolbar.

Either click on the down arrow beside the percentage and select an option from the drop-down menu, or simply place your cursor within the box and type in the percentage you want to zoom to.

Full Screen view

Full Screen view is the "no-frills" way to view your text. It hides all menus and toolbars, and is useful for when you want to work free of distractions.

To change to Full Screen view:

1. Click on **View** on the menu bar.

2. From the View pull-down menu, select **Full Screen**.

3. To return to the view mode you were using previously, click on **Close Full Screen** (depending on the version of Word you are using, it may be a button [as shown below] or the words "Close Full Screen" in a box), or press the Esc key on your keyboard.

Formatting

Once you have viewed your document, you will want to format it. To access Word's formatting features:

1. Select the text you wish to format.

2. Click on **Format** on the menu bar.

3. From the Format pull-down menu, select **Paragraph**. (Microsoft Word applies most formatting features to one paragraph at a time — the paragraph in which the cursor is situated — unless you have selected multiple paragraphs.)

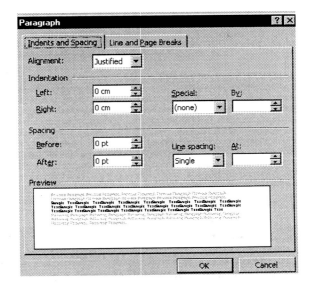

4. Make your formatting choices from the Paragraph dialog box (shown below). The options offered in this dialog box are described in the following sections.

Alignment (Justification)

Justification refers to the way text is aligned relative to the left and right margins. Chapter 3 explains justification and how to justify text using the formatting toolbar. Alternatively, text can be formatted in the Paragraph dialog box by selecting the desired justification from the Alignment drop-down menu.

Indentation

Indentation allows you to decrease or increase the distance of text from the left, right or both margins. Indents are shown on the ruler at the top of the page and are also visible as they are applied to text on the page.

Indentation indicators

Instructions for indenting text

1. Select the text you wish to indent.

2. Click on **Format** on the menu bar.

3. From the Format pull-down menu, select **Paragraph**.

4. Under **Indentation** in the Paragraph dialog box click on the up arrow beside the Left or Right margin text box to increase the indentation. (Click on the down arrow to decrease). The preview pane will show you how text will look with the selected indentation applied.

5. When you are happy with the appearance of the indentation, click on **OK**.

In the indentation section, you can also use the special indentation functions to achieve effects such as first line indentation and "hanging indents" (where the entire paragraph is indented *except* for the first line — this is often used to align bulleted lists.)

QUICK TIP

You can select the entire document by clicking on EDIT then clicking on SELECT ALL or hold down the CTRL key and press A (Ctrl+A).

EXERCISE — Justifying text using Word

❶Ms S.Law
PO Box 69
Harrogate
HG1 2YR

Gummy Confectionery
323-351 Gummy Rd
Manchester
M2 4AB

April 22, 1998

Dear Sir/Madam,

❷Please find enclosed a packet of Gummy Chocolates, which was purchased from your shop as a gift for Easter.

❸As you can see from this returned portion it is inedible. The

Gummies have the appearance of having been refrigerated or

they have spoiled.

❹ Perhaps a quality assurance glitch has occurred. We are looking forward to hearing from you on this matter.

Regards,

S.Law

❺P.S. We have been in contact with your customer service
department and they asked me to put it in writing.

❶ This text has been right justified (aligned with the right edge of the document).

❷ This paragraph is indented from both the left and right margins and is fully justified (aligned with both left and right edges of the document).

❸ The lines in this paragraph are spaced further apart vertically, as the line spacing has been set to 1.5 lines. This paragraph has also been indented on the right margin.

❹ A tab has been placed at the beginning of the sentence.

❺ This is a hanging indent.

Line Spacing

Line spacing allows you to adjust the vertical distance between lines. Increased line spacing is often used to make a document easier to read.

Instructions

1. Select the text you wish to format.
2. Click on **Format** on the menu bar.
3. From the Format pull-down menu, click on **Paragraph**.
4. From the Paragraph dialog box click on the arrow beside in the Line Spacing drop-down list box and select the spacing you want applied between lines of selected text.

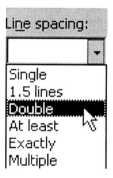

Options offered in the Line Spacing drop-down menu:

At Least: The At Least option allows Word to apply the minimum line spacing that it can to fit in larger fonts that cannot usually fit within the specified spacing.

Exactly: This choice forces Word to evenly space lines.

Multiple: Allows lines spacing to occur as a percentage. For example, multiple spacing of "2" is equivalent to 200% (that is, double line spacing).

Manual Page Breaks

Microsoft Word automatically separates your document into pages, beginning a new page when the current page is full. (Page breaks are shown in different ways, according to your view of the document. In Normal view, automatic page breaks are represented by a line of dots: .... In Page Layout view, each page looks like a separate piece of paper.)

Occasionally, however, you may want to begin a new topic on a fresh page before the current page is completely full. You can do this by inserting a manual page break.

Inserting a manual page break

1. Place the cursor where you want the page break to appear.

2. Hold down the **Ctrl** key.

3. Press **Enter**. In Normal view, the manual page break will appear as a series of dots, like an automatic page break, but the words "Page Break" will appear within the line of dots. In Page Layout view, you will see that Word has moved any text below the manual page break to a new sheet of on-screen paper.

Removing a manual page break

To remove a manual page break in Normal view:

1. Select the manual page break.

2. Press the **Delete** key.

Page Setup

The preferences set in Page Setup will affect the appearance of your entire document, such as margins, paper size, headers and footers (although each paragraph, section or word can be formatted individually — applying formatting to selected paragraphs is discussed in the following section of this chapter).

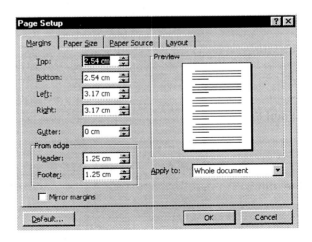

Instructions

To change the Page Setup settings:
1. Click on **File** on the menu bar.
2. From the pull-down menu, select **Page Setup**.
3. Under the margins tab, use the arrows beside each text box to increase or decrease the margin size (alternatively simply type in the desired margin size). Similarly choose header and footer margins.

Tabs

Tabs move text to preset distances on the screen, making it easy to align text, for instance to create tables and columns.

By default, Tabs in Word are set to approximately 1.27 cm (half an inch). You can change this distance to suit your needs.

Instructions

1. To create the headings such as in the example below type a heading, then press the Tab key to move to the next preset tab stop. Type the next heading and then press Tab again to move to the next tab setting.
2. Once the headings have all been entered press Enter to start a new line. Type in the next entry, then press Tab. The text will line up beneath the headings.

CARS FOR SALE

MODEL	YEAR	VALUE
Ford Orion GLX	1997	£12,500
Toyota MR2	1995	£18,500
Ford Fiesta	1994	£5,000

Changing Tab Defaults

To change the default (preset) distances and set your own tabs, follow these steps:
1. Click on **Format** on the menu bar.
2. From the Format pull-down menu, select **Tabs**.

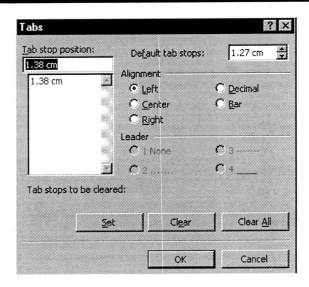

3. Click the mouse pointer inside the **Tab Stop Position** text box.

4. Enter the distance you wish to apply to tabs.

5. Just as you can justify paragraphs, you can choose to align text with the right or left edge, or with the centre, of each tab. Select the alignment; for example, left, centre, right, decimal or bar tabs. (The Bar tabs option inserts a vertical line at the tab stop, while the Decimal tab stop aligns the decimal point at the tab stop.)

6. Choose a leader if you wish. This will insert a printable character wherever tab is pressed.

7. Once you have made your choices, click on **Set**. To set several tabs repeat these steps, each time increasing the distance from the left margin. Once you have set all your tabs, click on **OK**.

Changing tab settings

1. Select the text for which you want to change the tab settings.

2. Click on **Format** on the menu bar

3. From the Format pull-down menu, click on **Tabs**.

4. In the Tab Stop Position list box, click on the tab you wish to change, then click inside the appropriate Alignment radio button or Leader radio button.

5. Click on the **Set** button.

6. Click on **OK**.

Deleting tab settings:

1. Open the Tabs dialog box (click on **Format**, then **Tabs**).
2. Select the tab you wish to remove from the list of tabs in the Tab Stop Position list box.
3. Click on the **Remove** or **Clear** button (depending on the version of Word you are using).
4. Click on **Close** or **OK**.

Reminder

If you have already aligned text using Tab, or if you set tabs before typing text, you must highlight the text before you can edit the tabs.

QUICK TIP

When working with tabs and indents, it is a good idea to turn on the Show All Characters mode. The characters that appear are visual aids only, and will not print. Places where you have pressed the Enter key will display ¶; spaces will be displayed as dots; and tabs will appear as arrows. These characters are handy to help you locate and, if necessary, delete spaces, extra lines and tabs.

To turn this feature on select Options from the Tools pull-down menu. Select the View tab, and check All in the Nonprinting Characters section. (To remove Show All Characters, simply uncheck the option by clicking on it again.)

Alternatively, click on the Show/Hide button on the toolbar (shown right).

Bullets and Numbering

Bullets and Numbering are an excellent way to make important points stand out or to emphasise lists of information.

These points are bulleted:

- This point has a bullet at the front.
- ❑ This point has a square bullet.

These points are numbered:

1. This point has a number placed at the front of it.
iv. This point has a Roman numeral.

Instructions

1. Select the text you wish to bullet or number.
2. Choose **Format** from the menu bar.
3. From the Format pull-down menu, select **Bullets and Numbering**.

4. From the Bullets and Numbering dialog box, choose the bullet or numbering option (as shown in figure 4.1 below) you wish to apply to your text.

5. From the tab marked Outline Numbering choose the structure of bullets and numbers you would like to apply to your document.

6. Click on **OK**.

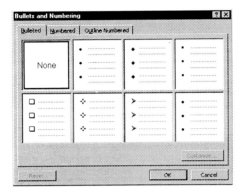 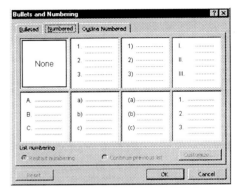

Figure 4.1: The Bullets and Numbering dialog box. Click on the appropriate tab to switch between bullets and numbers.

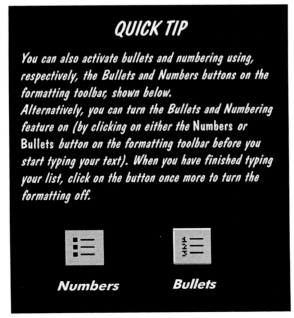
Borders and Shading

The Borders and Shading option lets you to make your headings and important points stand out.

To apply a border and shading to your text:

1. Select the text to which you wish to apply a border and shading.

2. Choose **Format** from the menu bar.

3. From the Format pull-down menu, select **Borders and Shading**.

4. From the dialog box (shown following), choose a **Border** option. There are many choices available when selecting a border. For

> *This has a border around it.*

> *This has a border and shading applied.*

instance, in the Settings sections of the dialog box you can change the appearance of your border, while the Style option allows you to choose a line style of your choice to apply to the border. Click OK once you have made your selections.

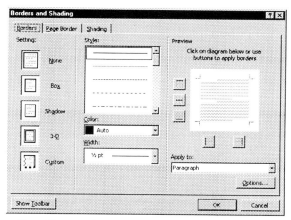

5. Click on the **Shading** tab to select a shading option. You can even choose a colour from the Fill colour palette to apply to the shaded area. Click on OK once you have made your selections.

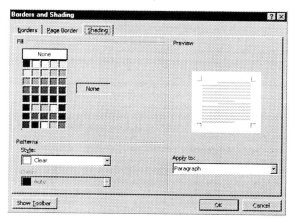

6. Click on OK to apply your choice to the selected text.

Chapter 5

Document-checking Tools

Word allows you to check the accuracy of your document before printing. You can check for spelling, grammar, or hyphenation, and even do a word count. If you have trouble finding just the right word, Word also has a thesaurus.

IMPORTANT NOTICE

Please note that the following dialog boxes will vary slightly between different versions of Word for Windows.

Spelling and Grammar Check

No matter how careful a typist you are, you may still miss typographical, spelling, or grammatical errors in your document.

Word can help you find and correct these errors using its spelling and grammar checking facilities. Word will suggest corrections when it notes an error, or unusual spelling or sentence construction.

Word 7 and 97 automatically spell check, placing a red squiggly line beneath unrecognised spelling, and in Word 97, a green line appears beneath unrecognised grammatical structures.

Instructions

To turn the automatic spell checker on, select **Options** from the **Tools** pull down menu. Under the "**Spelling & Grammar**" tab, check the box that reads "**Check spelling as you type**". To turn this option off, simply click inside the check box again to remove the tick. To turn the automatic grammar checker on or off, check the box that reads "**Check grammar as you type**".

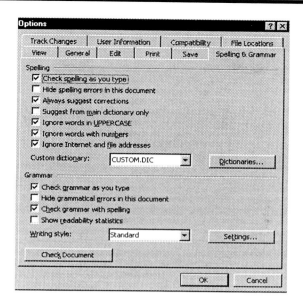

Language

Before beginning a spell check, it is important to note which language dictionary you are using. You may find the default is English (US) - American! To ensure that you are using the English (UK) language dictionary:

a) In Word 97: Place your pointer on **Language** from the Tools pull-down menu, then select **Set Language**.

b) From the Language dialog box select the language you prefer, then click on OK.

c) In Word 6 and 7: Click on Tools and from the pull-down menu select Language. From the "Mark Selected Text As" dialog box select the Language you wish to use, then click on OK.

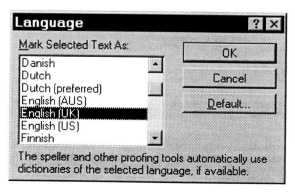

Instructions for spell checking (Word 97 users)

1. Click on **Tools** on the menu bar.
2. From the Tools pull-down menu, select **Spelling and Grammar**, as shown below:

A Spelling and Grammar dialog box opens.

Word 97 will search through the document and display words and sentences it considers incorrect in bold. In the Suggestions area of the box, Word 97 offers suggestions for correcting the selection.

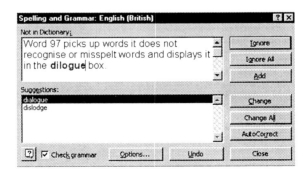

3. To accept a suggestion, click on it, then click on the **Change** button. If you choose **Change All**, Word will correct each instance of that mistake in the document.

4. To replace the mistake with something that isn't in the list of suggestions, simply type the change in the text box and click the **Change** button.

5. If you *don't* want to change the selection (for example, if you have deliberately used a nonstandard spelling), click on **Ignore**. To ignore that particular spelling or grammatical inconsistency wherever it appears in the document, choose **Ignore All**.

6. If you are using a word consistently throughout a document and Word marks it as "Not in Dictionary", you may want to add it to Word's list of recognised words. To do this, simply click on the **Add** button.

7. At any time you wish to go back one step or undo the last step, simply click on the **Undo** button.

8. When Word is finished checking the document, a dialog box appears notifying you that the check is complete. Click **OK** to return to the document.

Correcting grammar using Word's grammar-checking facility is similar. Incorrect sentences are displayed in bold, and word offers alternatives in the Suggestions text box. For instance, in the example below the section marked as incorrect by Word contains extra spaces.

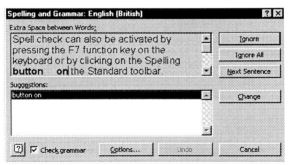

Instructions for spell checking with Word 6 and 7

1. Click on **Tools** on the menu bar.

2. From the Tools pull-down menu, select **Spelling**.

3. A Spelling dialog box opens. If a word is incorrectly spelt, Word displays it in the text box marked "Not in Dictionary" and offers suggestions for correcting the misspelt word.

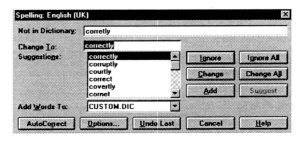

4. To correct a word, select the correctly spelt word from the Suggestions list and click on **Change**. If a word is misspelt more than once in a document, clicking on **Change All** corrects it throughout the document.

5. If you do not want to change the selected word, choose **Ignore**. If you click on **Ignore All**, Word will not display the same word again.

6. If the correct spelling is not displayed in the Suggestions list box, you can type the spelling you want in the Change To text box.

7. If you *don't* want to change what you've written (for example, if you've deliberately used a nonstandard spelling), click on **Ignore**. The **Ignore All** button will instruct Word to ignore that particular spelling or grammatical inconsistency wherever it appears in the document.

8. If you are using a word consistently throughout a document and Word displays it as being "Not in Dictionary", you may add it to Word's list of recognised words by clicking on **Add**.

9. To undo the last correction. Click on **Undo Last**.

10. When Word is finished checking the document, a dialog box opens notifying you that the check is complete. Click on **OK** to return to the document.

Instructions for using grammar checking with Word 97

1. Click on **Tools** on the menu bar.

QUICK TIP

There are three shortcuts to accessing Word's spelling and grammar functions:

1. *You can activate the Spelling and Grammar option by pressing F7.*

2. *You can access the spell checker by clicking on the Spelling button on the toolbar.*

3. *You can also correct a word using the right mouse button. Simply click on the misspelt word with the right mouse button, then select the correct word from the pop-up menu using your left mouse button.*

2. From the Tools pull-down menu, select **Grammar** (if installed).

3. If a sentence contains a possible grammatical error, Word displays it in the Sentence box and offers alternatives in the Suggestions box, shown below:

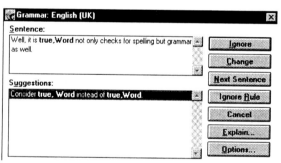

4. If you want an explanation of the suggestion, click on **Explain**. A Grammar Explanation window opens containing information about the grammatical error Word has noted. To close this window, click on the Close button (marked with an "X") in the top right-hand corner of the window.

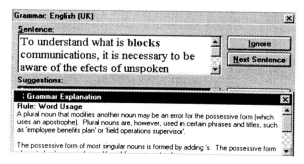

5. Click on **Change** if you want to change the sentence, or on **Ignore** to leave it as it is.

6. Click on **Next Sentence** to view the next sentence with possible grammatical errors.

7. Once the grammar check is finished, a Readability Statistics dialog box is displayed. Click on **OK** to close this window and return to your document.

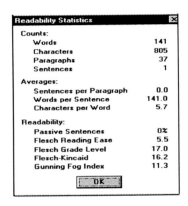

Thesaurus

Word's built-in thesaurus lets you search for synonyms or words related to your text.

Instructions

1. Select the word for which you wish to find a synonym.

2. Click on **Tools** on the menu bar.

3. Word 97 users, point to **Language**, then select **Thesaurus** from the Language pull-down menu. Word 6 and 7 users, select **Thesaurus** from the Tools pull-down menu.

4. The thesaurus dialog box opens, showing the **Looked Up** word and a list of suggestions in the **Replace with Synonym** box. If there are multiple meanings in the Meanings list box, select each meaning to view a new list of synonyms.

> **QUICK TIP**
>
> *You can also activate Word's Thesaurus by highlighting a word, holding down Shift and pressing the F7 function key.*

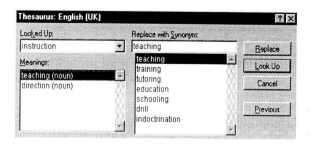

5. To see more words with similar meanings, click on a word in the Re-place with Synonym list box or in the Meanings list box and click on the **Look Up** button.

6. To change the highlighted word in the document choose a word from the Replace with Synonym list box and click on **Replace**.

7. If you decide not to change the word after all, click on **Cancel** to return to your document.

Hyphenation

When a document is justified, there may be too much blank space left between words, giving it a ragged look. You can solve this and smooth out the appearance of your document using the **Hyphenation** command, which will break up words, reducing the amount of blank space between them.

Instructions

1. Ensure that you are at the beginning of the document by using the vertical scroll bar to scroll up or pressing the Page Up button on the keyboard until you are on the first page. Now select **Tools** from the menu bar.

2. In Word 97, point to **Language**, then from the Language pull-down menu, click on **Hyphenation**. In Word 6 and 7, select **Hyphenation** from the Tools pull-down menu.

3. In the Hyphenation dialog box, click inside the **Automatically Hyphenate Document** check box as shown in the diagram on the following page. This will hyphenate your entire document where appropriate. If you later add text to your document, Word will hyphen-ate as you type.

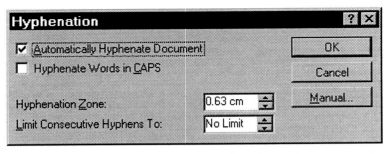

4. If you do not wish to hyphenate capitalised words, ensure that the **Hyphenate Words in CAPS** box is not checked. In addition, make sure that the **Limit Consecutive Hyphens To:** option is set to "No Limit". This controls the maximum number of consecutive lines of text that can end with a hyphen.

Word Count

The Word Count tool provides useful statistics about your document: including the number of pages, words, characters, paragraphs and lines.

Instructions

1. Click on **Tools** on the menu bar.
2. From the Tools pull-down menu, select **Word Count**.
3. The Word Count dialog box opens, showing the statistics of your document. To close the dialog box and return to your document click on **Cancel** in Word 6 and 7, or **Close** button in Word 97.

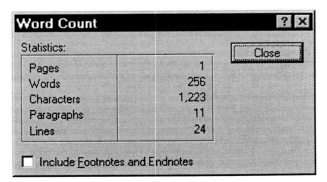

Chapter 6

Headers and Footers

Headers and footers are used to display information (such as your company's name and address, or the page number) at, respectively, the top or bottom of every page.

The Header and Footer function is located in the View pull-down menu. To insert a header or footer in your document:

Instructions

1. Select **View** from the menu bar.

2. From the View pull-down menu, click on **Header and Footer**.

   A toolbar appears on your screen and the text on your page becomes grey. This means that — for the moment — you can only access the header or footer of your document. The header and footer areas of your page are outlined by a dashed box (this outline will not print — it is simply shown to guide you).

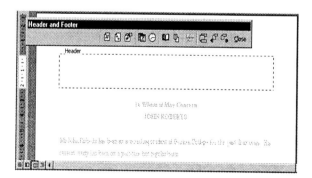

3. Type the text you would like to appear in the header or footer directly in the space provided. You can format the text as you would text in the body of your document. You can also customise your header or footer using the Header and Footer toolbar, discussed below.

4. To return to your document, click on the **Close** button on the Header and Footer toolbar.

The Header and Footer Toolbar

The most commonly-used buttons on the Header and Footer toolbar are discussed below:

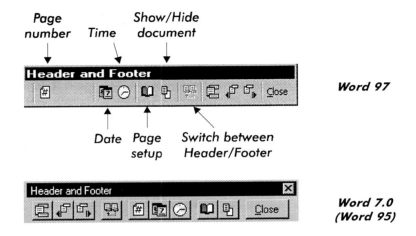

Word 97

Word 7.0
(Word 95)

Page Number

The Page Numbers function automatically numbers every page. If you copy, move, or insert pages the number is adjusted automatically.

Date and Time

Either of these buttons will insert the current date or time in your header or footer. (If you place both the date and time in your header or footer, insert a tab or space between them to make the text easier to read.) The date and time are updated whenever you save, close, open, print or copy your document.

To insert a date that *doesn't* change – for example, you may want to indicate that the document is a transcript of a meeting that took place on October 26 — manually type the date rather than using the toolbar button.

Page Setup

The Page Setup button allows you to determine how your headers and footers will appear on each page.

You can choose to have odd (usually right-hand) and even (usually left-hand) pages look different. For example, you can choose to right-justify the page numbers of odd pages, and left-justify those of even pages.

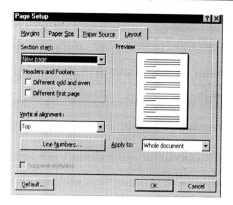

This is achieved via the Different odd and even button, which then displays the header and footer boxes on odd-numbered pages as "Odd page header" and "Odd page footer".

Similarly, the boxes on even-numbered pages read "Even page header" and "Even page footer".

In the Page Setup dialog box you can also choose to make the header or footer on the first page different to those used in the rest of the document (for example, you may not want a page number to appear on the first page). This is achieved via the Different first page button, which will change the header and footer boxes on the first page to read "First page header" and "First page footer".

Show and Hide Document

This option switches between displaying the body of your document in a dimmed grey or not showing it at all when you are editing headers and footers. Click on this button to hide your document until you click on it again.

Switch between Header and Footer

To switch quickly between the header and footer of a page, use the Switch between Header and Footer button. If the cursor is in the header, it will move to the footer, and vice versa.

Close

Clicking on the Close button returns you to your document.

Deleting

To remove or edit a header or footer, position your cursor inside the dashed area, select the text you want to remove, and press either the Delete or the Backspace key.

Chapter 7

Printing

Despite the promises of the office-technology pioneers, the day of the "paperless office" is still far off. Paper documents (often called "hard copy") continue to be a vital part of professional communications and record-keeping.

Word offers a number of features that make printing your document easy:

Print Preview

Print Preview allows you to see the layout of your page as it will appear on when printed. This gives you the opportunity to make changes before you print.

Instructions

1. Click on **File** on the menu bar.
2. From the File pull-down menu, choose on **Print Preview**.
3. Click on **Close** (in Word 97) or **Cancel** (in Word 6 or 7) to return to your document.
4. You can also print preview your document by clicking on the **Print Preview** button on the toolbar.

Print Preview Toolbar

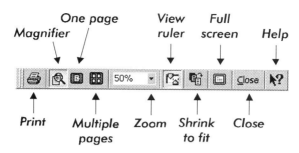

The buttons on the Print Preview toolbar are discussed below:

Print

Click on this button to send your document directly to the printer.

Magnifier and editing

Using the magnifier you can zoom in to your document to see fine details.

When the magnifier is turned off (by clicking on the button so that it no longer appears depressed) you can edit your document in Print Preview mode. A blinking cursor will appear on your page instead of a magnifier, and text can be edited as usual. To return to magnify mode, click on this button once again.

One Page

Click on this button to view pages one at a time.

Multiple Pages

Click on this button to preview several pages at once. Simply click on this button once, then on the drop-down menu drag your cursor across the grid shown to select the number of pages you want to view.

Zoom

To view your document at a different magnification, enter a value between 10 and 200 in this box.

View Ruler

This button either hides or displays the ruler, which can be used to change margins, paragraphs or other settings.

Shrink to Fit

If only a small amount of text appears on the final page of the document, clicking on this button will shrink the text to fit on the previous pages. This is especially useful if only the signature of a letter spills onto the last page.

Full Screen

Full screen allows you to view more of your document by hiding most the screen elements. To reveal screen elements, click on Esc.

Close

Click on this button to close the print preview toolbar and return to your document view.

Help

If you need help with any of the buttons, simply click on Help followed by the button you are not sure of. A message will pop-up explaining the purpose of that button.

The Print Command

Wicon hen you are satisfied with your document, you can print out a hard copy using the Print command.

Instructions

1. Click on **File** on the menu bar.

2. From the File pull-down menu, select **Print**.

3. From the Print dialog box choose one of the following options:

   a) To print the entire document, click on All (in the Page range section).

QUICK TIP

Clicking on the printer icon on the Standard toolbar sends your document directly to the printer without opening the Print dialog box.

b) To print the page you are currently editing (that is, the page in which the blinking cursor is currently situated), click on the **Current page** button in the Page range section.

c) To print selected pages of your document, click inside the **Pages** button in the Page range section. In the Pages text box, type the numbers of the pages you want to print: for example, to print pages 1 to 5, type: 1-5

To print pages 2 and 4, type: 2,4

To print pages 1, and 5 to 10, type: 1,5-10

d) To print more than one copy of the selected pages, enter the number of copies you wish to print in the "**Number of copies:**" section, or use the arrows to select a number, then click on OK.

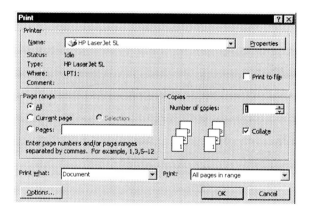

Note that in the screen shot above the option **Selection** is displayed in a lighter shade of grey to the other options, meaning that it is currently not available.

Selection is used to print only a certain portion of a document, such as a single paragraph. To do this, select the paragraph or text you want to print, then choose **Print** from the **File** pull-down menu, click inside the Selection radio button and click on OK.

Paper Size

Before printing, check that the paper size of your printer is set to match the specifications of your document (which were set via Page Setup). If these are not the same, you may have difficulties printing.

To check the paper size your printer is set to, click on the Properties button in the Print dialog box. A dialog box showing your printer's properties opens. Under the Paper tab select the appropriate paper size, and click on OK.

You will notice many other printing options in the Properties dialog box – many of these are useful and it is a good idea to spend some time experimenting with them.

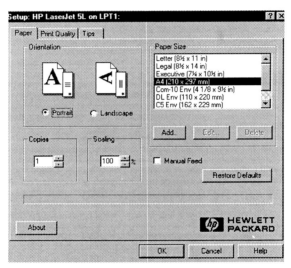

Word 6 and 7: Print dialog box

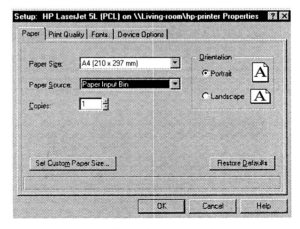

Word 97: Print dialog box

Chapter 8

Putting it All Together

Are you ready for the challenge of creating a document? This chapter will guide you step-by-step through preparing the memorandum shown on page 70, using many of the skills you have learned in previous chapters.

Launching Word and Creating a Document

1. Launch Microsoft Word. Each time you launch Word, a new document, titled Document1, is automatically created.
2. If you do not have a new document open, hold down Ctrl and press "N" to open one.

Toolbars

Before typing the memorandum, make sure that both the standard and formatting toolbars are open. If you cannot see the toolbars, do the following:

1. Click on **View** on the menu bar.
2. From the View pull-down menu, select **Toolbars**.
3. Make sure that the words **Standard** and **Formatting** are checked. If they are checked, there will be a tick in front of the words. If the words are not checked, simply click on the words **Standard** and **Formatting** to select these options. Remember you should always have these two toolbars available on your screen.

Page View

It is important to choose a page view before typing your document, so that it will appear on the screen in the way you expect. To change to Page

MEMORANDUM

To: All Staff

From: Managing Director

Date: (Insert current date)

Subject: Company Celebration

There is a point at which production becomes counterproductive. J and J Corporation wants our management and staff to strike a balance between work and play by getting together for a party this Friday from 6.30 pm.

Please leave your

- Calculators
- Computers
- Management theories
- Paperwork; and
- Suits

at home. But remember to bring your family and friends along.

Hope to see you all there.

Layout view (the view that most closely resembles the final, printed document), do the following:
1. Click on **View** on the menu bar.
2. From the View pull-down menu, click on **Page Layout**.

Entering and Editing Text

1. Type the word MEMORANDUM (using either the Shift or **Caps Lock** keys to access capital letters).

2. Press the **Enter** key three times.

3. We will work in centimetres while creating this document. If your ruler is not set to centimetres, follow these steps to change the units of measurement:

   a) Click on **Tools**.

   b) Select **Options** from the Tools pull-down menu.

   c) From the Options dialog box, click on the tab marked "**General**".

   d) In the "**Measurement units**" section, click on the down arrow and select "centimeters".

4. To begin creating the tabbed introductory lines, click on **Format** on the menu bar.

5. From the Format pull-down menu, select **Tabs**.

6. In the Tabs dialog box, type **5** inside the Tab Set Position text box.

7. Make sure the radio button under Alignment is set to **Left**.

8. Click on **OK**.

9. Now type the text as follows:

   a) Type "To:", press the Tab key to move the set distance, then type "All Staff".

   b) Press the Enter key twice to begin a new paragraph and create a line between paragraphs. Type "From:", press the Tab key to move the set distance, then type "Managing Director".

   c) Press the Enter key twice. Type "Date:", press the Tab key to move the set distance, then type the date.

   d) Press the Enter key twice. Type "Subject", press the Tab key to move the set distance, then type "Company Celebration".

   e) Press the Enter key four times.

QUICK TIP

To ensure your document looks the way you intend it to, view it using Page Layout mode. (Click View, then select Page Layout).

Now type the following paragraph: (Remember, it is not necessary to press Enter at the end of the first line as Word automatically applies text-wrap.)

There is a point at which production becomes counterproductive. J and J Corporation wants our management and staff to strike a balance between work and play by getting together for a barbecue this Friday from 6.30 p.m.

10.   Type the rest of the document by following the instructions below:

   a) Type "Please leave your", press the Enter key twice.

   b) Type the following words, pressing the Enter key once between each: "Calculators", "Computers", "Management theories", "Paperwork, and", "Suits".

   a) Press the Enter key twice, then type "at home. But remember to bring your family and friends along."

   c) Press the Enter key twice, then type "Hope to see you all there."

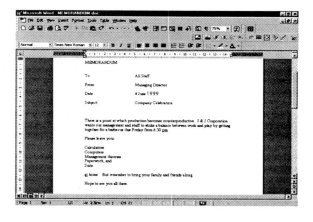

11. Position your cursor (the "I" beam) in front of the word "barbecue" and press the Delete key eight times or until the word "barbecue" is deleted. (Alternatively double-click on the word and press the Delete key once.)

12. Type the word "party".

Saving

It is a good idea to save your work now, so it will not be lost in case of the unexpected (such as a power failure or an unintended computer shut down).

1. Click on **File** on the menu bar and select **Save** from the pull-down menu.

2. Since this document has not been saved before, the Save As dialog box will appear. We'll call this file "Party", so in the **File Name** text box, type "Party".

3. Click on **Save** or **OK** to save the document. The name "Party" should now appear on the title bar.

Formatting Your text

Now that you have entered your text, it is time to begin formatting it.

1. Move your pointer to the selection area (the left margin of the document) and click the mouse three times to select the entire document. (Alternatively, select the entire document by positioning your cursor or the "I" beam in front of the word "MEMORANDUM" and, while holding the left mouse button, drag the mouse across and down the page (or simply click on **Edit** then **Select All** from the Edit pull-down menu). Once you have selected the entire document the typing will appear as white letters on blocks of black.

2. Click on the down arrow in the Font Name section of the formatting toolbar.

3. From the drop-down list box, select **Arial**. (Note the font names are in alphabetical order).

4. From the Font Size drop-down list box (shown at right), select 12 to change the text to 12 point.

5. Click on the **Justify** button on the Formatting toolbar to fully justify the document (that is, set the text flush with both the left and right margins).

6. You have finished making global formatting changes. Click anywhere on the page to de-select the text.

7. To format the word "MEMORANDUM", first select it by placing the "I" beam in front of the word in the selection area and clicking the mouse button once.

   Alternatively, position your cursor in front of the word and, while holding the left mouse button down, drag across it.

8. Click on the **Bold** button on the formatting toolbar (see diagram below). Then click on the **Centre** button to centre the heading.

   Click anywhere on the page to de-select the word.

9. Position the mouse pointer in front of the word "Calculators" and, while holding the left mouse down, drag down and select the following five lines (ending with the line reading "Suits"), as shown below:

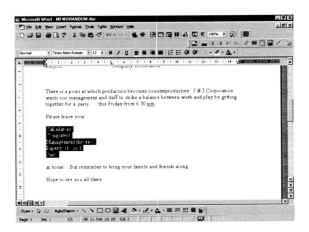

10. Click on **Format** on the menu bar.

11. From the Format pull-down menu, select **Paragraph**. A Paragraph dialog box opens.

12. Under the Indentation tab, in the Left text box, click on the up arrow to increase the indentation to 2 cm.

13.   Click on **OK** to apply this indentation to your selected text.

14.   Make sure the text is still selected and click once on the **Bullets** button on the formatting toolbar. A bullet will appear in front of each point.

15.   Now we want to add emphasis to the last line of the memorandum. To select the text, position the mouse pointer in the selection area to the left of the last line and click the left mouse button once.

16.   Using the formatting toolbar, change the font size to 16, make the text bold and centre it.

17.   Click on the **Save** button to save the changes you made. Notice the Save As dialog box does not open up as the document has already been named.

Spelling and Grammar Check

Your document now needs to be checked — this is an important step, as a well-checked document looks professional and creates a favourable impression.

1. Select **Tools** from the menu bar.

2. Word 97 users should select **Spelling and Grammar** from the Tools pull-down menu. (Alternatively, press F7 to activate the Spelling and Grammar check.)

   To activate the grammar check Word 6 and 7 users should select **Tools** from the menu bar, then choose **Grammar** from the Tools pull-down menu.

3. A dialog box opens listing the incorrectly spelt words in the Not in Dictionary text box.

4. Change incorrectly spelt words by choosing the correct word from the Suggestions list box and clicking on **Change**.

5. If the correction you want is not listed in the Suggestions list box, manually correct the word in the Change To text box, then click on **Change**.

6. If you do not want to change a word, click on **Ignore** or **Ignore All**.

7. Sentences with incorrect grammar will be displayed in the dialog box with a suggested alternative. Click on **Change** to accept the alternative, or choose **Ignore** to leave the sentence as it is.

8. Once the spelling and grammar check is complete, click on **OK**.

Hyphenation

To apply hyphenation:

1. Click on **Tools** on the menu bar.
2. Word 97 users should point to **Language** and select **Hyphenation** from the Language pull-down menu. Word 6 and 7 users should select **Hyphenation** from the Tools pull-down menu.
3. Click on the **Automatically Hyphenate Document** check box.
4. Click on **OK**.
5. Click on the **Save** button on the standard toolbar to save the changes.

Printing

It is useful to preview your document before sending a copy to the printer. To do this:

1. Click on **File** on the menu bar.
2. From the File pull-down menu, select **Print Preview**.
3. If you are happy with the layout, click on the **Printer** button on the Print Preview toolbar to print the document, then click on **Close** to return to your document. (If you are not happy with the layout, click on **Close** without printing to return to your document and make any changes.)

Closing the Document

1. Click on **File** on the menu bar.
2. Click on **Close** from the File pull-down menu. If for some reason you have not saved your changes, while closing your document a dialog box will open up asking you if you want to save changes. Click on OK to save changes before closing the document.

QUICK TIP

There are two other easy ways to open a document. Either choose File from the menu bar and click on the filename at the bottom of the pull-down menu, or select Open from the File pull-down menu then click on the filename from the Open dialog box.

Opening the Document

You may want to make changes to your document after you've closed it. To re-open the document:

1. Click on the **Open** button on the Standard toolbar.

2. In the Open dialog box, under the Name section, click on the document titled "Party" to select it.
3. Click on **Open**.

Leaving Microsoft Word

Once you have finished word processing, you will want to exit Word. To do this:

1. Click on **File** on the menu bar.
2. Select **Exit** from the File pull-down menu.
3. If any changes have not been saved, a dialog box will appear asking if you want to save changes to the document.
4. Click on **Yes** to save the document and exit Word.

Congratulations on completing this exercise successfully!

Chapter 9

Columns

One way to make your document easier to read, especially if it includes a large amount of text and few graphics, is to format the text in columns, such as the text in the example below.

Instructions for setting columns

Before setting columns, ensure you are in Page Layout view. To change to Page Layout view, select **Page Layout** from the View pull-down menu.

1. Select **Format** from the menu bar.

2. From the pull-down menu, click on **Columns**. The following dialog box appears.

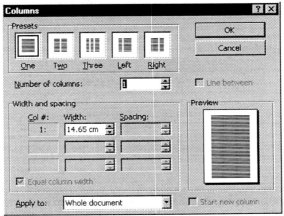

3. From the Columns dialog box, choose an option from the **Presets** section or use the arrows to select the number of columns.

4. To change or adjust the column width, uncheck the **Equal column width** box by clicking inside it. When this box is unchecked, you can change the column width and spacing by clicking on the up or down arrows. (If this box remains checked Word will automatically adjust the columns so that they remain the same width.)

5. Click on **OK**.

6. On your document you will notice that the ruler splits so that each column has its own ruler. When you reach the bottom of a column, any text you type will automatically flow into the next column.

Inserting a Column Break

Text that is typed in columns will automatically flow from the bottom of one column to the top of the next. However, if you wish, you can specify at which point in the text you would like to begin a new column by inserting a column break.

Instructions

1. Place the insertion point at the position in the text where you want the column to break.

2. Select **Insert** from the menu bar.

3. From the Insert pull-down menu, click on **Column break**.

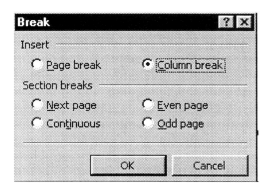

4. Begin typing text in the new column. To insert another column break in the second column, follow the same procedure.

Varying Columns Within Text

Within the same document you may wish to place some text in columns and other text in normal format (you will see this layout used in many newsletters).

Instructions

1. Once you have typed the text you want in column format, click on **Format** on the menu bar.
2. Select **Columns** from the Format pull-down menu.
3. Select **One** column from the Preset section.
4. In the "Apply to:" section, click on the down arrow and select **This point forward** from the options listed. For instance, in the diagram below the first part of the text is set in three columns, while the second section has been set in a single column using the "This point forward" option.

Applying Columns to Selected Text

You can also apply columns to selected text once you have finished typing your document. To do this, follow the instructions below:

Instructions

1. Type your entire document.
2. Select the paragraph or points you want to format in columns.
3. Click on **Format** on the menu bar.
4. Select **Columns** from the Format pull-down menu.
5. Choose an option from the Presets or change the number of columns yourself. (Notice the Apply to section reads "Selected text").
6. Click on **OK**.

Chapter 10

Tables

Tables are used to display text in a rows and columns. Tables can help you organise and present large amounts of information so that it is easy to read and understand. They can also enhance the overall look of your document.

Tables consist of rows (horizontal) and columns (vertical). Each "box" in the table is called a cell.

	Column1	Column2	Column3
Row1	Cell 1,1	Cell 1,1	Cell 1,1
Row2	Cell 2,1	Cell 2,2	Cell 2,3
Row3	Cell 3,1	Cell 3,2	Cell 3,3
Row4	Cell 4,1	Cell 4,2	Cell 4,3
Row5	Cell 5,1	Cell 5,2	Cell 5,3

Creating a table

1. Decide how many columns and rows you will need in your table. (Don't panic if you find later on that you need more: you can always add them.)
2. Click on **Table** on the menu bar.
3. Choose **Insert Table** from the Table pull-down menu. A dialog box will appear, as shown in the following diagram:

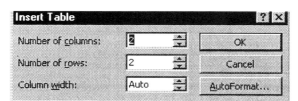

4. Type in the number of columns and rows you want (or use the up and down arrows).
5. Click on OK.

You can quickly create a table from the standard toolbar. Simply click on the Tables *icon and* drag, holding down the left mouse button to select the number of columns

Entering text into a table

1. Click inside the cell you wish to type in, and type in the text as usual. The cells will change size as you type to accommodate your text. Just as when you are typing text in the body of the document, you can format justify text inside a table.

2. To move around within the table, you can either use the mouse to click in the cell you want, use the arrow keys to move from cell to cell, or press the Tab key to move across the row (pressing Tab at the end of a row will move the cursor to the beginning of the next row).

Editing the Table

Ensure that your cursor is inside the table before you edit it.

Inserting Rows or Columns

1. Select a row or column by placing your cursor in front of the row in the selection area or on top of the column and clicking the left mouse button once.

2. Click on **Table** on the menu bar; from the pull-down menu, choose **Insert Cells, Insert Rows** or **Insert Columns**. Word always inserts a row *above* the selected row, and inserts a column to the *left* of the selected column.

Removing Columns

To remove columns:

1. Click inside any cell in the row or column you would like to delete.

2. Click on **Table** in the menu bar.

3. From the pull-down menu, select **Delete cells**. A dialog box will appear.

4. Click on Delete entire row or Delete entire column. Then Click on **OK**.

NOTE:

If you delete or remove entire columns or rows, all the text inside these columns or rows will be deleted.

Changing Row and Column Widths

Adjusting the size of your rows and columns is easiest with the mouse.

1. Carefully move your mouse between the columns or rows. Notice that it will change to a double-headed arrow with two dividing lines in-between as it crosses cell boundaries, as shown below.

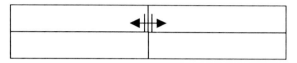

When you cross a column boundary, the dividing lines are vertical; when you cross a row boundary, the dividing lines are horizontal. Aim for a column boundary when you want to change column width, and aim for a row boundary when you want to change row height.

2. When you see the double-arrow pointer, hold down the left mouse button and drag left or right to change column width, or up or down to change row height.

Borders and Shading

Borders and shading can help you group information within a table more clearly (for example, shading the first row and column to make it more clear that they serve as row and column headings, or putting a border around the cell that contains the total of a column of figures).

Word 97 automatically puts borders around every cell in a table to form a grid. Word 6 and 7 do not put the borders in; it is up to you to put them in if you want them.

Adding borders and shading

1. Select the sections of the table for which you want borders or shading.
2. Click on Format on the menu bar.
3. Choose Borders and Shading from the Format pull-down menu.
4. Click on the Borders tab from the Borders and Shading dialog box and choose the border style, line style and colour you want. (If you want to

print a coloured border, you will need a colour printer. If you don't have one, stick to black borders, as coloured borders can sometimes print out in unpredictable shades of grey on a black-and-white printer.)

5. If you want shading, click on the **Shading** tab on the **Borders and Shading** dialog box and choose the percentage of shading and the appropriate colour. The higher the percentage, the darker the shading. (Again, if you only have a black-and-white printer, use the various shades of grey for your shading, rather than colours.)

Removing Borders

1. Click anywhere inside the table, then click on **Select Table** from the Tables pull-down menu.
2. Click on the **Borders** button from the formatting toolbar.
3. Click on **No Borders**.

Removing Shading

1. Click anywhere inside the table, then click on **Select Table** from the Tables pull-down menu.
2. Click on **Borders and shading** on the formatting menu bar.
3. Click on the **Shading** tab on the Borders and Shading dialog box.
4. Click on the **None** box, then click on **OK**.

Chapter 11

Graphic Effects

It is easy to make your documents visually compelling using the options offered by Microsoft Word. You can stylise text using WordArt, insert ready-made Clip Art pictures, or create your own pictures using Word's drawing tools.

WordArt

WordArt is used to stylise and emphasise text to draw attention to your document. The words below have been stylised using WordArt.

Inserting WordArt
Instructions for Word 6 and 7

1. Position your cursor in the position where you would like the WordArt to appear.
2. Choose **Insert** from the menu bar.
3. From the Insert pull-down menu, choose **Object**.
4. Scroll through the "Object type" options until **Microsoft WordArt** is displayed. Click on this option once to select it, as shown in the following diagram.

Figure11.1: The words above have been stylised using WordArt.

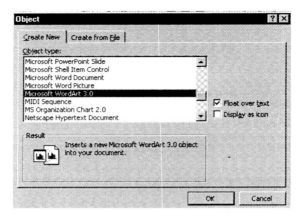

5. Click on **OK**.

6. Your screen will now become the Microsoft WordArt screen:

7.   In the floating dialog box (labelled "Enter Your Text Here") type your text.

8.   Click on **Update display** from the floating dialog box to view your text.

9.   Format the text using the WordArt formatting toolbar, shown in figure 11.2 below.

10.   To select the shape of your text, click on the **Plain Text** drop-down box.

11.   Spend some time exploring the WordArt toolbar (shown in figure 11.2) to get a feel for the options it offers.

QUICK TIP

When using WordArt it is often a good idea to select Best Fit as the font size and click on the Stretch to Frame option. Choosing these options allows your text to stretch to the width of the frame when resized.

12. When you are happy with the appearance of your text, click on a blank area of the page to exit the WordArt screen and return to your document.

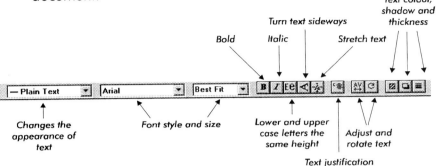

Figure 11.2: The WordArt Formatting toolbar

Instructions for Word 97 users

1. Click on the Insert WordArt button (shown at right) from the **Drawing** toolbar, situated at the bottom of the page. (If you cannot see the toolbar, click on View, then Toolbars, then Drawing. A tick should appear in front of "Drawing" on the drop-down menu to show the toolbar is activated.)

2. From the WordArt Gallery (shown below), choose a preferred style.

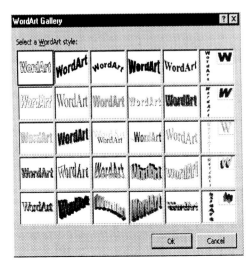

3. Click on **OK**. The Edit WordArt Text dialog box appears, as shown in the diagram below:

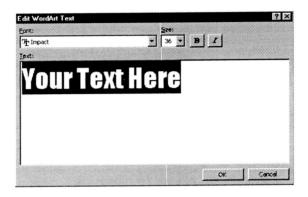

4. In the space provided, enter your text.
5. Click on **OK**. The WordArt will appear on your document. To move it into position, click-and-drag using the mouse.

Resizing WordArt, Pictures and Shapes

You may need to change the size of a WordArt object, a picture or a shape so that it fits in your document.

1. Click once on the WordArt, picture or shape so that a box appears around the image.
2. On the outline of the box (the "Frame Edge") you will see small squares (shown in the diagram below), called handles. As the mouse cursor moves over a handle you will notice it changes to a double-headed arrow.

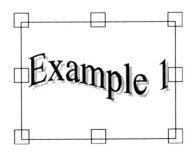

3. Hold down the left mouse button and drag up, down, left or right to resize your WordArt object or picture. To resize proportionately, drag using a corner handle.

4. To return to your document click once on a blank area of the page.

Deleting WordArt, Pictures or Shapes

1. Click once on the WordArt object, picture or shape so a box appears around the image.

2. Press the **Delete** key.

Clip Art

It can be difficult for your document to attract attention when you are working only with text. Microsoft Word enables you enhance your document with pictures, using a feature called Clip Art.

Inserting Clip Art

1. Position your cursor on the page where you would like the picture to appear.

2. Select **Insert** from the menu bar.

3. Click on **Object** from the Insert pull-down menu.

4. Select **Microsoft Clip Gallery** from the Object dialog box (or other clipart format). The Insert Picture dialog box will appear.

5. From the list of category names, click on the name of the picture you wish to use, or click on the picture so that it has a square around it.

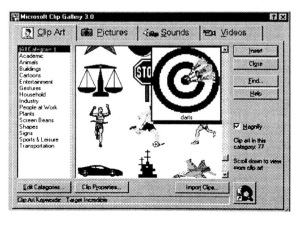

6. Once you have chosen a picture, click on **Insert** to place it in your document.

The Drawing Toolbar

Using the Drawing toolbar you can draw pictures directly in your document. To access this toolbar:

1. Click on the **Drawing** button on the standard toolbar.
2. The Drawing toolbar appears on your screen. (The Word 97 Drawing toolbar is shown in figure 11.3, below, while the Drawing toolbar visible in Word 6 and 7 is shown over the page, in figure 11.4.)

The Pick Tool

(Note: This is called the "select object" tool in Word 97). This tool allows you to select the shapes you have created in order to make changes to them.

Creating and Inserting Shapes

1. Click on the desired shape button from the Drawing toolbar.
2. Place the cursor in the document where you want the shape to appear.
3. Hold down your left mouse button to insert the shape, and, *without lifting your finger from the mouse button*, drag the shape to the size you want it.
4. Lift your finger off the mouse button. The shape will remain.

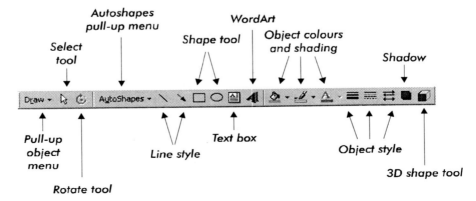

Figure 11.3: The Word 97 Drawing toolbar.

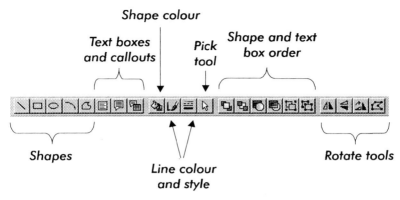

Figure 11.4: The Drawing toolbar in Word 6 and 7.

Shape Colour, Line Colour and Line Style

Using the tools offered by Microsoft Word, you can change the thickness, style and colour of lines and shapes once you have drawn them.

Filling a shape with colour

1. Click once on the shape you want to change. Small squares will appear around your selection.
2. From the Drawing toolbar, click on the **Fill Color** tool button.
3. Click on the colour you want; for more choices, click on **More Fill Colors** or **More Line Colors**.

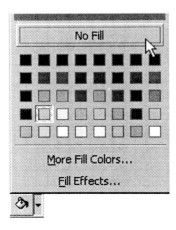

Instructions for using Line Color

1. Click once on the line you want to change. Small squares will appear around your selection.

2. From the Drawing toolbar, click on the **Line Color** button.

3. Click on the colour you want; for more choices, click on **More Line Colors**.

4. To change the line style, make the line active, then click on the **Line Style** button and choose the appropriate line style.

5. Click on **OK**.

Text Boxes

The text box button lets you draw a floating text box on your page. Text boxes are great for adding floating captions to pages, such as placing names on maps.

> **This is a floating text box**

1. Click on the **Text Box** button on the Drawing toolbar.

2. Draw a box on your page by holding down the left mouse button and dragging.

3. Type text into this box.

4. You can add a shadow to the box to enhance its effect using the instructions above for applying a shadow to a shape.

> This is a floating
> text box with a
> shadow applied

5. To remove the border or shadow in Word 6 or 7, choose white as the colour for both the border and shadow. In Word 97 choose "No line" and "No shadow" from the Line Colour and Fill Colour options respectively.

Shape and Text Box Order

The Order option allows you to decide the order in which shapes or text boxes should be arranged; that is, which should be placed in front of which.

Instructions for Word 97 users

1. Select the shape or text box you want to work with using the pick tool or cursor.

2. From the Drawing toolbar, select **Draw**, then **Order**.

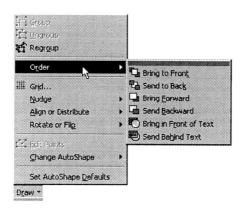

3. Click on an option. **Bring to Front** and **Send to Back** move the object to the front or back respectively. **Bring Forward** and **Send Backward** move the object forward or backward one "layer" at a time. **Bring in Front of Text** and **Send Behind Text** determine whether the text will appear to overwrite the object, or whether the object will be superimposed on the text.

Instructions for Word 6 and 7

1. Using the Pick tool, click on the shape or text box to be ordered.

2. Click on any of the Order buttons depending on what you wish to do. **Bring to Front** and **Send to Back** move the object to the front or back respectively. **Bring Forward** and **Send Backward** move the object forward or backward one "layer" at a time. **Bring in Front of Text** and **Send Behind Text** determine whether the text will appear to overwrite the object, or whether the object will be superimposed on the text. In the example below, the oval has been brought to the front, while the rectangle has been sent to the back.

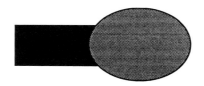

Freeform Tool

The Freeform drawing tool allows you to draw freehand shapes, just as if you were scribbling with a pen on a piece of paper.

1. In Word 97, click on **AutoShapes** from the drawing toolbar, then select **Lines**, followed by the Freeform tool as shown in the diagram below. Word 6 and 7 users, click on the Freeform tool on the drawing toolbar.

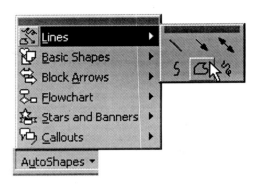

2. Move the mouse cursor to the position on the page where you would like to begin drawing, then click the left mouse button.

3. Move the mouse to create each side of the freeform shape, clicking the left mouse button at each corner.

4. Double-click when you are finished drawing.

Shadows

Using Word's Shadow option a variety of shadows can be placed behind any shape.

1. Select the shape by clicking on its outline once with the left mouse button.

2. Click on the **Shadow** option on the Drawing toolbar, as shown at right.

3. From the Shadow drop-down menu, select the type of shadow you want applied to the shape.

QUICK TIP

Any item on the Start Menu which has a little arrow to the right-hand side indicates a 'cascading menu' containing other items. These automatically unfold whenever your mouse alights on that item.

Callouts

Callouts are specially-shaped text boxes and pointers that emphasise the text within them.

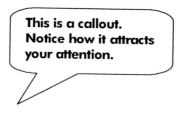

1. In Word 97, from the Drawing toolbar select **AutoShapes**, then **Callouts**. In Word 6 and 7, open the drawing toolbar and click on the **Callout** button.

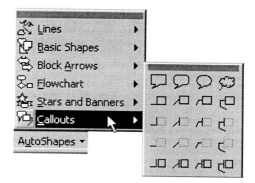

2. From the **Callout** window, click on the callout you want.
3. You will notice that your pointer has become a small cross. To draw the callout box, hold down the left mouse button while dragging your mouse across the page. Release the left mouse button when your callout is the desired size.

   (You can adjust the size of the callout at any time by selecting it, then moving the pointer over the outline until it changes to a double-headed arrow. While holding the left mouse button down, move this arrow to resize the callout.)
4. A cursor will appear in the callout. Type your text in the box.

Note

Users of Word 6 and 7 can change the look of callouts by clicking on the "Text-callout properties" button beside the Callout button.

Rotate buttons

The rotate tools allow you to spin (rotate) and flip your shapes.

1. Select the shape you want to rotate by clicking on it once.

2. Click on the rotate tool to rotate or flip your shape. (Word 6 and 7 users, refer to the Drawing toolbar in figure 11.4 for information on the rotate buttons).

3. Small square "handles" will appear around the outline of the selected shape.

Place the mouse pointer on one of these handles and, while holding down left mouse button, rotate the object to the desired angle.

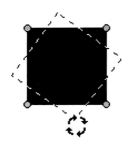

Chapter 12

Macros

Macros are a great way to automate tasks you perform often. For example, you can use a macro to bold, underline and change a font name and size in a single step. In this chapter you will learn how to set up special keystrokes to perform macros (this is called "assigning a macro to your keyboard").

Setting up a macro is straightforward, but it does require several steps. By following the steps one at a time, you will learn not only how to set up the macro in the example below, but also how to apply macros to your own tasks.

Recording a Macro

This example explains how to set up a macro that bolds, underlines, and changes the font and size of text all at once.

Step 1: Preparation

1. Make sure Word is running, then open a new document.

2. Type some text.

3. Position the cursor in the selection area to the left of your text and click the left mouse button once to select the text. (You can select the text using the keyboard if you prefer).

Step 2: Naming and Describing the Macro

A macro is a series of Word instructions which is saved as a single command. Using a Macro helps you avoid repetitive tasks.

In order to use a Macro it will need to be given a name and saved. It is also a good idea to give the Macro a description so that you can easily recognise its functions when you want to use it next.

Instructions for Word 97 users

1. Click on **Tools** on the menu bar.

2. Point to **Macro** from the Tools pull-down menu, and click on **Record New Macro.**

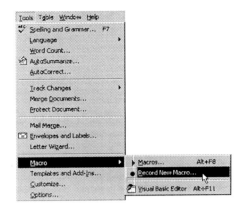

3. In the Macro Name text box, type a name for the macro.   In this example, type **Format** as the macro name (as shown below).

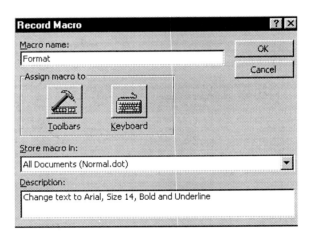

4. Click in the **Description** section and type a brief description of the macro you are going to record. The description is optional but it is advisable to enter a description to recognise your macros. In this example, type **Change text to Arial, Size 14, Bold and Underline** (see figure above).

5. Click on the **OK** button.

> ### QUICK TIP
>
> *Always follow the correct procedure when exiting Word. That is, click on File then Exit. Do not simply turn your computer off while Word is still on screen.*

Instructions for Word 6 and 7

1. Click on **Tools** on the menu bar.

2. From the Tools pull-down menu, select Macro.

3. In the Macro Name text box, type a name for the macro. In this example, use Format as the macro name.

4. Click in the Description section and type a brief description of the macro you are going to record. In this example, type Change text to Arial, Size 14, Bold and Underline.

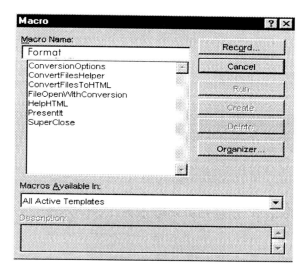

5. Click on the **Record** button.

Step 3: Assigning your Macro

The next step is to designate which keystrokes to use to run the macro. This is called "assigning" the macro.

Instructions (all versions)

1. In the Record Macro dialog box, click on the **Keyboard** button under the "Assign Macro To" section. Word will record the keystrokes that you use to activate your macro, so that those strokes will run the Macro.

   Alternatively, you can assign a Macro to a menu item or toolbar button from which you can run your macro by clicking on the toolbar item or menu item respectively.

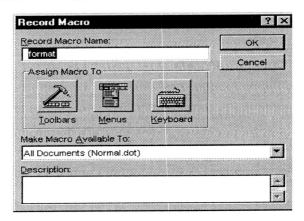

2. In the Customize dialog box, position your cursor in the "Press New Shortcut Key" text box, then hold down the **Alt** and **Ctrl** keys together and press **F12**.

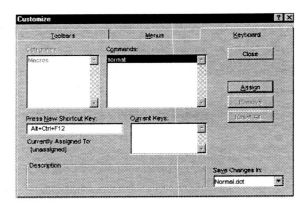

Note: The message **Currently Assigned To: (unassigned)** will appear beneath the text box to inform you that these keys are currently not assigned to any Word functions. Therefore, you are free to use them for your macro. You cannot assign key combinations that are already in use by Word (such as Ctrl+S or Ctrl+X) to your macro.

NOTE

Alternatively, you can run a macro by selecting the text you want to affect, selecting Macros from the Tools pull-down menu, clicking on the macro name and then on the Run button.

3. Click on the **Assign** button. Notice that **Alt+Ctrl+F12** is listed in the Current Keys text box.

4. Click on the **Close** button. A Macro Record button dialog box appears on your screen, usually in the upper-left corner of the document. The button on the left of this dialog box is the Stop button, while the button on the right is the Pause button.

Step 4: Recording your Macro

At this point, Word begins acting like a recorder, keeping track of all the menu choices, button clicks, and typing you do and storing them in your macro.

1. Click on the **Font Name** drop-down list box and change the font name to **Arial** (just as you would do so ordinarily when formatting text).

2. Click on the **Font Size** drop-down list box and change the size to **14**.

3. Click on the **Bold** button, then on the **Underline** button.

4. Click on the Stop button on the **Macro Record** dialog box to stop recording your steps.

Step 5: Running the Macro.

In your macro named "Format", you have stored the formatting procedure required to change the font to 14-point Arial, and to add bold and underlining. At any time you can now run this macro by following the instructions below:

1. Type some text — for example:

   The hair on the napes of their necks rose as fear overcame them. So far, nothing strange had happened nor had they witnessed any strange sighting. Now, they waited with bated breath for what they were about to encounter.

   (Make sure this text is in a different font from Arial, 14-point size, so that you can watch your macro at work!)

2. Select the text.

3. Hold down the **Alt** and the **Ctrl** keys at the same time and press **F12**.

4. The macro will run, changing the font and text style to 14-point Arial, bold and underlined.

Deleting a Macro

If you no longer need a particular macro, delete it by following the steps below:

1. Select **Tools** from the menu bar.

2. In Word 97, from the Tools pull-down menu, point to **Macro**. From the Macros pull-down menu click on **Macros....** In Word 6 and 7, select **Macros** from the Tools pull-down menu. A dialog box will open.

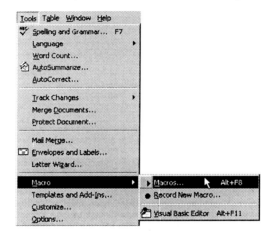

3. Under the Macro Name text box, click on the macro you want to delete: in this example we will delete the macro named **Format**.

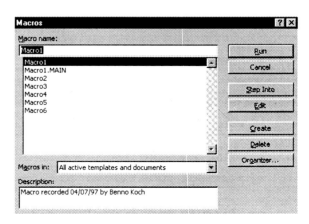

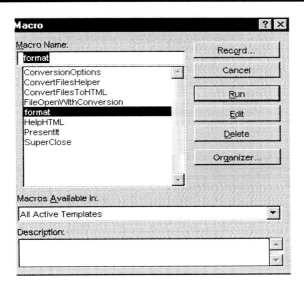

4. Click on the **Delete** button.

5. A message will appear asking whether you want to delete the macro; click on **Yes**.

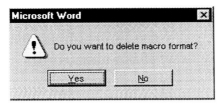

6. Click on the **Close** button (which is situated in the top right-hand corner of the window and marked with a small "X").

Chapter 13

Merging Documents

Mail merge allows you to type a standard letter and merge with it with a large number of addresses. This saves you considerable time as you do not have to reproduce the letter several times.

You can also combine, or "merge", the standard letter with other information, such as account balances or expiration dates.

Merging involves two documents:

1. **Main document:** This is the standard information that forms the basis of your final, merged document.

2. **Data document:** This document contains the variable information (such as names and addresses) that combines with the main document.

There are three steps to using Mail Merge: creating the main document, creating the data document, and merging the two.

Step 1: Creating the Main Document

1. Click on the **New** button on the Standard toolbar to open a new document.

2. If you are not in Page Layout View, click on **View** on the menu bar and select **Page Layout**.

3. Type the letter below, exactly as shown. (Remember to insert the current date and then press the Enter key two times before typing "Dear".)

(Insert Date)

Dear

Enclosed is a new price list for your information. Please do not hesitate to contact me if you have any questions.

I look forward to doing further business with your company.

Yours faithfully

Peter Williams
Managing Director

---

4. Save the document, naming it **Client**.

5. Click on **Tools** on the menu bar and select **Mail Merge** from the Tools pull-down menu.

6. A Mail Merge Helper dialog box opens up. Click on the **Create** button.

7. From the Create drop-down list box, select **Form Letters**.

8. Click on the **Active Window** button to make the **Client** document the main document.

Note: The type of merge and the name of the document now appear in the "Main document" area (under the Create button) of the Mail Merge Helper dialog box, as shown below:

Step 2: Creating the Data Document.

The data document contains the information that varies between copies: in this example, we will use a list of customer names and addresses as our data document.

1. Click on the **Get Data** button in the Mail Merge Helper dialog box.

2. Select **Create Data Source** from the drop-down list box.

3. A **Create Data Source** dialog box opens, displaying commonly used field names. A field is a piece of information, such as a name, a sub-urb, a postcode or an account number. The field names in the list form the basis of information in your data document.

4. Remove any of the suggested field names you do not want to use by clicking on them and then clicking on **Remove Field Name**. For example, to remove the City field, click on "City", then on the **Remove Field Name** button.

   Similarly, you can add field names by typing the new field name in the Field Name text box, then clicking on the **Add Field Name** button.

5. When you have only field names that you want to use, click on the **OK** button on the Create Data Source dialog box.

6. A **Save As** dialog box appears, requesting a file name. You need to save the data document before you can start entering the names and addresses.

7. Name the data document **Database**, then click on the **Save** button to save the data document.

8. Another dialog box appears, informing you that the data document you have saved contains no records. (A record is a set of field entries

that go together: for example, a person's name and mailing address.) In other words, your data document is empty.

9. Click on the **Edit Data Source** button to add new records to the data document.

10. Enter three records using addresses of friends or made-up addresses in the Data Form dialog box . To move from one text box to another, press either the Enter key or Tab.

11. When all the data is entered for the first "customer", click on the **Add New** button to move to Record 2.

12. Once you have entered the information, click on the **View Source** button on the Data Form dialog box. This displays the records you just entered in the form of a table, as shown below:

13. Be sure to save the records you have just entered by clicking on the **Save** button on the toolbar.

Step 3: Merging the Documents

1. Click on the **Mail Merge Main Document** button to return to the main document named **Client**.

2. Note that a third toolbar has now been added to the **Client** document. This is the Mail Merge toolbar. The small arrow button on this toolbar which points towards the left will show the previous record, the button beside this shows the first record, the button with an arrow pointing towards the right will display the next record, and the button to the right of this will display the last record. The number in the box indicates the number of records.

3. Click on the **Insert Merge Field** button on the Mail Merge toolbar.

4. You need to specify where each field will appear in the final document. To do this, follow the steps below:

    a) Create the "name" line: From the **Insert Merge Field** pull-down menu, click on **Title** then press the spacebar once; click on the **Insert Merge Field** button, click on **FirstName**, and press the spacebar once; click on the **Insert Merge Field** button and click on **LastName**.

    b) Press the Enter key once to move to the next line.

    c) Next, click on the **Insert Merge Field** button, then click on **JobTitle** and press the Enter key once.

    d) Click on the **Insert Merge Field** button, then click on **Company** and press the Enter key once.

e) Click on the **Insert Merge Field** button, then click on **Address1** and press Enter key once.

f) Click on the **Insert Merge Field** button, then click on **Address2** and press Enter key once.

g) Click on the **Insert Merge Field** button, then click on **State** and press the spacebar once; click on the **Insert Merge Field** button, then click on **Postal Code**, and press the Enter key once.

5. Position the cursor after the word "Dear" and do the following:

a) Click on **Insert Merge Field** button, click on **Title** and press the spacebar once.

b) Click on **Insert Merge Field** button, then click on **LastName** and press the spacebar once.

6. Click on the **ABC** button to see a preview of the merged document. Make sure you click on this button again before you decide to print a copy of the merged document — if you do not you will only be able to print the page you are currently viewing. To print the entire merged document turn the ABC button off.

7. Click on the **Check for Errors** button to check the merged document for any errors (such as wrong address and missing field names) which may have occurred while merging.

8. Click on the **Merge to New Document** if you wish to create a third document using all the merged records. For example, if you have 100 records merged with your main document, this button tells Word to create a new document consisting of a hundred versions of the main document.

9. If you do not wish to create a new merged document, you can send the merged versions directly to the printer by clicking on the **Merge to Printer** button.

10. Click on the **Save** button to save the main document (in this case, **Client**), then close the document.

11. You will find that the data document (in this case, **Database**) is still open. Close the data document.

MSWord "Cheat Sheet"

Task	Shortcut
Creating a new file	Hold down the Ctrl key and press the letter "N".
Opening a file	Hold down the Ctrl key and press the letter "O", then follow the screen prompts.
Saving a document	Hold down the Ctrl key and press the letter "S". If this is the first time you've saved the file, type a name in the File name box, then press Enter. Once you have named your file, Ctrl+S will update your changes.
Selecting text	Position the cursor beside the text you want to select. Hold down the Shift key and press the arrow keys (left, right, up or down). OR press the F8 function key twice to select a word, three times to highlight a sentence, four times to highlight the whole paragraph and five times to select the entire document.
Cut, Copy and Paste	Select text, choose either **Cut** (hold down Ctrl and press the letter "X") OR **Copy** (Ctrl+C). Position the cursor in the new location and re-trieve your selection by holding down Ctrl while pressing the letter "V" to **Paste**.
Undo or Redo	To **Undo** hold down Ctrl and press the letter "Z". To **Redo** use Ctrl+Y.
Help	Press F1.
Spell Checking	Press F7 and follow on screen prompts.
Printing	Hold down Ctrl key and press "P", then follow the on screen prompts.
Finding text	Hold down Ctrl and press the letter "F", then follow the screen prompts.

The Complete Beginner's Guide to Windows 95

This book isn't for the sort of people who get all frisky at the thought of a new operating system. They're already running Windows 95 and have been since day one. As the title suggests, it is for beginners:

- ❑ If you've just bought a new PC it will almost certainly be running Windows 95. You may need a helping hand to get started, and this book will serve as your introduction to Windows 95.
- ❑ If you've been using a PC with DOS or an earlier version of Windows and have decided to take the step up to Windows 95 this book will be a steadying hand to the new and to the different.
- ❑ If your office, school or college requires you to use a Windows 95 computer, this book will quickly show you the basics so you can get on with your work.
- ❑ Even if you're already using Windows 95 but simply want to do more with it, this book will teach you some neat tricks.

ISBN: 1-873668-28-7

Price: £4.95

About the Author

David Flynn is closely connected with Microsoft through his computer consultancy activities and is currently beta-testing early versions of the next Windows upgrade.

The Complete Beginner's Guide to Windows 95 is a low-cost, easy to understand guide, specially designed for everyone who hates wading through hundreds of pages of information to find a simple answer. **Order form on page 112**

Create Your Own Electronic Office

Home-based business... Cottage industry... Small Office/Home Office (SOHO)... whatever term you use, operating from home, means you escape the stresses, pressures and overheads of a busy town centre office. What-is-more, the time saved by not having to commute will allow you to work more efficiently and spend quality time enjoying yourself.

If this sounds like the kind of independence that you have dreamed of, then this book is for you. With its help, you will:

- ● Decide whether working from home is for you;
- ● Equip your office with the right technology to make it efficient from day one:
- ● Plan your new business and working environment

£5.95

Included are chapters on getting yourself motivated for working by yourself for yourself, how to maintain a healthy separation between your work and private life, and how to present yourself and your new business in a professional manner.

Find What You Want on the Internet

The sheer size of the Internet's information resources is its biggest challenge. There is no central repository of all this information, nor it is catalogued or sorted in ordered fashion.

Find What You Want on The Internet is designed to teach Internet users — from novices to veterans — how to locate information quickly and easily.

The book uses jargon-free language, combined with many illustrations, to answer such questions as:

- Which search techniques and Search Engines work best for your specific needs?
- What is the real difference between true 'search' sites and on-line directories, and how do you decide which one to use?
- How do the world's most powerful Search Engines really work?
- Are there any 'special tricks' that will help you find what you want, faster?

ISBN: 1-873668-48-1
Price: £5.95

There is also a bonus chapter covering Intelligent Agents — special high-tech personal search programs that can be installed on your computer to search the Internet on your behalf, automatically.

Create Your Own Web Site

The World Wide Web is being transformed into an important business and communications tool. Millions of computer users around the globe now rely on the Web as a prime source of information and entertainment.

Once you begin to explore the wonders of the Internet, it isn't long before the first pangs of desire hit – you want your own Web site.

Whether it is to showcase your business and its products, or a compilation of information about your favourite hobby or sport, creating your own Web site is very exciting indeed. But unless you're familiar with graphics programs and HTML (the "native language" of the Web), as well as how to upload files to the Internet, creating your Web page can also be very frustrating!

£5.95

But it doesn't have to be that way. This book, written by an Internet consultant and graphics design specialist, will help demystify the process of creating and publishing a Web site. In it you will learn:

- What free tools are available that make producing your own Web site child's play (and where to find them);
- How to create your own dazzling graphics, using a variety of free computer graphics programs;
- Who to talk to when it comes to finding a home for your Web site (If you have an Internet account, you probably already have all that you need).

Tax Self Assessment Made Easy

Like it or not, the biggest change to the UK tax system has taken place. Self assessment is already in place for many taxpayers who may not even know it. Can it be ignored? No! New requirements for keeping records for example, or changes in the date for submitting tax returns will affect NINE MILLION people according to The Revenue. Penalties for not keeping records can be £3,000, whilst late tax returns can be charged at up to £60 per day.

Thankfully, Stefan Bernstein has distilled all the jargon down to a simple easy to follow guide **at a price the ordinary taxpayer can afford.** The book tells you what you have to do and when to do it, warning you of what happens if you don't.

ISBN: 1-873668-09-0   **Price:** £5.99

The Complete Beginner's Guide to The World Wide Web

Scott Western, an acknowledged, British, World Wide Web expert, leads you through every aspect of THE WEB highlighting interesting sites, and showing you the best ways to find and retrieve the information you want. Discover:

- ✔ How to minimise your time on-line, saving you money
- ✔ Professional tricks for searching the Web
- ✔ How World Wide Web pages are designed and constructed
- ✔ All about domain names and getting your own web space   **Price:** £5.95

Making Money on The Internet

In 1996, businesses clocked up more than £350 million in sales over the Internet. Within one year that figure had risen to £500 million and was still growing almost exponentially!

These on-the-net businesses used the Internet to slash costs; decrease the cost of customer support; reduce purchasing costs; cut marketing expenses and to reach hitherto untapped markets. Their secrets are revealed in this book, so that you can make money on the Internet before your competitors beat you to it.

You'll find answers to the following questions:

- ● Is the Internet right for my business?
- ● How can I use the Internet to get and keep customers?
- ● Can I get started quickly and cheaply?
- ● What are the potential problems?   **Price:** Only £3.95

"highly recommend"
"An excellent publication."
Business Opportunity World

The Complete Beginner's Guide to The Internet

What exactly is The Internet? Where did it come from and where is it going? And, more importantly, how can everybody take their place in this new community?

The Complete Beginner's Guide to The Internet answers all of those questions and more. On top of being an indispensable guide to the basics of Cyberspace,

❑   It is the lowest priced introduction on the market by a long way at a surfer-friendly £4.95. Who wants to spend £30+ on an alternative to find out The Internet is not for them?

❑   It comes in an easy-to-read format. Alternatives, with their 300+ pages, are intimidating even to those who are familiar with The Net, let alone complete beginners!

Price: £4.95

The Complete Beginner's Guide to The Internet tells you:

* What types of resources are available for private, educational and business use,
* What software and hardware you need to access them,
* How to communicate with others, and
* The rules of the Superhighway, or 'netiquette'.

Book Order Form

Please complete the form USING BLOCK CAPITALS and return to
TTL, PO Box 200, Harrogate HG1 2YR or fax to **01423-526035**

❑ I enclose a cheque/postal order for £_____ made payable to '**TTL**'

❑ Please debit my Visa/ Amex/Mastercard No:

Book	Qty	Price

Postage: Over £8 free, otherwise please add 50p per item within UK, £1.50 elsewhere **Total:**

Expiry date:

Signature:

Date:
Please allow 14-21 days delivery.

We hope to make you further exciting offers in the future. If you do not wish to receive these, please write to us at the above address.

Title: _____ Initials: _____

Name: _____

Address: _____

_____

_____ Postcode: _____

Daytime Telephone: _____

wordwin